Looking 4 Love...

IF YOU SEARCH FOR HIM WITH ALL YOUR HEART YOU WILL FIND HIM-
DEUTERONOMY 4:29

---

in all the wrong places

Kamekio Danielle Lewis

AuthorHouse™
1663 Liberty Drive
Bloomington, IN 47403
www.authorhouse.com
Phone: 1-800-839-8640

©2010 Kamekio Danielle Lewis. All rights reserved.

No part of this book may be reproduced, stored in a retrieval system, or transmitted by any means without the written permission of the author.

First published by AuthorHouse 1/22/2010

ISBN: 978-1-4490-7322-0 (e)
ISBN: 978-1-4490-7321-3 (sc)

Printed in the United States of America
Bloomington, Indiana

This book is printed on acid-free paper.

This book is intended solely for inspirational and informational purposes. Please consult a licensed psychologist or a mental health professional if you are seeking expert advice. All scriptures are referenced from the Holy Bible (New International Version).

If you look for Him with all your heart you will find Him
Deuteronomy 4:29

Acknowledgements

First, I want to thank God for giving me the courage to write this book. I embrace His love and I hold on to the assignments which He has placed on my life. This was not in my plan, but God has intervened my plans with His agenda. I thank Him because every delay has worked to my advantage! I want to thank all the people who have imparted so much wisdom in my life and helped me grow so much spiritually. I would like to thank my husband, Dennis for all his love and support. I want to also thank Pastor Jimmy Talley and the Mt. Sinai COGIC family (Camden, Arkansas) for providing me with foundational scriptures and encouraging words through the years. Apostle Sidney P. Malone and the New Growth family (Memphis, TN), thank you for delivering and ministering the applied word of God, which has allowed me to prosper in every area of my life, mentally, physically, spiritually, and financially. I have learned the importance of forgiveness, I have learned how to forgive and I am practicing my love walk!

I want to thank my dear mother, Dora Green for her many sacrifices throughout the years. Her tenacity to fight each fight has taught me that without faith it is impossible to please God, for if you come to God you must believe that He is, and that He is a rewarder of them that diligently seek Him (Hebrews 11:6). I thank her for teaching me the true meaning of hard work and the importance of education. I want to thank Horace Green, my step-dad, who has always been the glue that held us all together. His devotion to our family has always been genuine and pure. I want to thank my sisters Lakisha Jones and Tyronda Welch for always having a listening ear and for putting up with my strict rules and radical viewpoints. To my brother, Tyrone Welch, I love you and I thank you for always challenging me to be the best me. I thank the best in-laws in the world, Dennis and Emma Ashford; you have always treated me with love and kindness. To my number one brother-in-law, Navarette Ashford, thank you for all your kind words. To my best friend, Lavonne (McLilly) Hamby, thanks for always believing in me. I love you like a sister. I also want to thank my friends Chiffone Shelton and Betina Hunt for helping me, praying with me, and keeping me grounded.

Thank you to all the friends, family, and co-workers who have greatly impacted my life. I now know that we all had to cross paths for destiny to be fulfilled. You have all impacted my life greatly.

A special thanks to my editor and friend Idrissa N. Snider.
IsArt Productions
www.idrissansnider.com

Dedications

 I am dedicating this book to the love of my life, Dennis Lewis. I want to thank you for believing in me, thank you for supporting me, and most of all thank you for loving me. Thank you for showing me what love is and how true love feels. Thank you for teaching me how to love me and for helping me get through some very difficult times.

 To my children, Kaveyon & Kemareyon Lewis. I love you so much. Thank you for your love and support. I struggled so long with finding the right man and trying to find someone to love me. God has blessed me with three men that give me enough love to last three life times. You are my greatest accomplishments!

Forward (Lavonne Hamby)

I am honored that I was asked to write the forward for my best friend's book. I highly respect and love her; she is such an intelligent and wonderful person. She has always been very creative. As little children we always dreamed of writing books, though I know she never thought it would be under these circumstances. Fortunaly what the devil meant for bad God turned it into Good.

Abuse is a very private and hidden topic in many women lives. What she has done in writing this book has exposed many things about her self that even people that are very close to her did not know about. Kamekio had to learn to deal with the pain of her past, but most of all she realized that she had not forgiven. Through the years and through the tears she has been holding on to and harboring ill feelings. I think it took a lot of courage and lover for her to expose so many personal issues and private battles, especially when other people see you as beautiful, confident and such a strong woman. I pray that this book touches and sows several seeds in the lives of women all over the world, helping them to heal and to forgive.

I personally have never been in an abusive relationship and sometimes can't believe that she has. This part of her life did help to shape her to be who she is today and to help her spread God's word about how to overcome the pain of your past! This book is her testimony and it shows us how God can bring you out of any bad situation. I now understand how some women feel when they don't have a father or a father figure in their lives and why they search for that love in all the wrong places. My pastor has always said that we live and we die by the choices we make. In the end of this journey, she made the choice to live. She decided that she wanted to live a more productive and spirit filled life, so she had to make better and much wiser choices. With God's help she was able to overcome the abuse. God loved her through this and God love s you….

Contents

Acknowledgements		vii
Dedications		ix
Forward (Lavonne Hamby)		xi
Chapter 1:	Tell It Like It Is	1
Chapter 2:	Living in my past	5
Chapter 3:	My Friend: *Grace & Mercy*	19
Chapter 4:	Why Me?	25
Chapter 5:	Choices	31
Chapter 6:	Shacking	35
Chapter 7:	No more Pretending	43
Chapter 8:	The Signs	59
Chapter 9:	Daddy's little girl	63
Chapter 10:	Looking for love	79
Chapter 11:	Starting Over	87
Chapter 12:	Forgiveness	95
Chapter 13:	A New Day!	105

Precious Promises:

God is love. Whoever lives in love lives in God, and God in him. In this way, love is made complete among us so that we will have confidence on the Day of Judgment, because in this world we are like him. There is no fear in love. But perfect love drives out fear, because fear has to do with punishment. The one who fears is not made perfect in love. We love because he first loved us. If anyone says, "I Love God," yet hates his brother, he is a liar. For anyone who does not love his brother, whom he has seen, cannot love God, whom he has not seen.
(1 John 4:16-20)

A woman's abuser threatened to shoot her in the head and then attach the protection order to the hole in her head.
-Arkansas

Today staff attended a funeral of a woman who had been killed by her husband.
- California

Today a woman who had been abused for almost two years filed an emergency protection order. She said, "I want the hurt to stop."
– Oklahoma

A woman in a very abusive situation dropped her restraining order against her abuser because she knew that without him, she would not be able to pay the rent.
- Massachusetts

Domestic Violence Counts 2008 – A National Network to End Domestic Violence

Domestic Violence hotlines are a lifeline for victims in danger, providing support, information, safety planning, and resources.

Her Story

*I got flowers today.
It wasn't my birthday or any other special day.
Last night we had a fight and he hit me,
But I know he is sorry
Cause I got flowers today.*

*I got flowers today.
It wasn't our anniversary or any other special day.
Last night he threw me against the wall and started to choke me,
But I know he's sorry,
Cause I got flowers today.*

*I got flowers today.
It wasn't Mothers day or any other special day.
I was so swollen and bruised I was ashamed to answer the door.
But I know he's sorry,
Cause I got flowers today.
If I leave him, where will I go?
What about money? What about my kids?
It's getting worse every time but I'm afraid to leave.
But I know he's sorry.
Cause I got flowers today.*

*I got flowers today.
My family and friends filed by to see me
Asking why I never left him,
If I only had the strength and courage to, but I didn't.
So I got Flowers today.*

Copyright© Sept 91 Allen "Two Trees" Dowdell

Chapter 1

TELL IT LIKE IT IS

I share with you what I think and how I feel. I share with you all in the name of keeping it real. I came to you to talk to you about my messed up situation. I needed your support and your compensation. I came to you, yet you ignored me. You ignored my thoughts and my feelings. I came to you to talk to you about my messed up situation and you minimized my dedication. I came to you and you mocked my feelings and added insult to my injuries. I came to you and you talked to me like I was incapable of a loving relationship and you treated me like I was a child. I came to you and you told me how wrong I was, yes how wrong I was for loving him. You tried to convince me of the right thing to do and the right way to go. You told me all of the reasons that I should leave, but you didn't understand how badly I wanted to stay. I needed you to comfort me, but you only told me what you thought I should do and what you would do if you were me. You completely ignored my feelings, which were all so true. I needed you to listen to me, to hear me, and to understand these feelings that were running through my mind and racing through my heart. You didn't listen. You never listen. You just couldn't understand how important this love was to me and you overlooked my feelings because they seemed to be... to be stupid to you, to be crazy to you, to be wild and foolish to you, yet I was oh so passionate about this contaminated love. I did not realize how wild and foolishly I was living as I jeopardized my life for this strife. A lot of people said that I was crazy; yes I was crazy in love. I looked for this love and I found this love, but this love it didn't love me back. "Are you mad at me because I decided to stay?" Yes, I did stay, but then I left, and then somehow I went right back. I returned to him because all the time while you were so mad at me he was comforting me. All the time when you were mad at me and ridiculing me, he was giving me a glimpse of hope and a sense of security. Look at you, you sit there and you judge me, but you don't know me. I was content with this imitation of love. In my mind, I thought that I needed this love, I accepted this love, yet I continued to look for this love. You wanted me to detach from this love and you tried to force me to see the reality of this love, but I could not because I did not want to see. I did not want to see how toxic this relationship had become. I was in love with a love that didn't love me.

"Tell It Like It Is", is a mental snapshot, of how I felt many years ago. I am sure that there are other women that share these same feelings as they sit in the middle of their storm. I will tell you this story, because it is my story. And though you may not completely understand my circumstances, I pray that it will help you to see your situation clearly as you move toward the healing process. My sincere hope is that women will began the move from being the victim to being victorious! We will celebrate our victories together, as we overcome many difficult situations. I expose a lot of hurt and pain, but stay focused on my healing and my transformation, because I have gotten past all the guilt and the shame. Yes, the pain was real. The guilt and the shame were also very real, but the recovery has been much greater for me. I have learned how to move forward with my life. I pray that this book empowers and encourages you to move on with your life and helps you to learn how to forgive. If you or a someone you know is an abusive relationship, I hope that you are able to learn some valuable lessons from my past mistakes. I trust that you will consider getting help individually or collectively, to improve your situation. I know that I have been made free and this abuse will never be a part of my life again. This thing that once had a very strong hold on my life, has actually allowed me to grow and develop in so many areas. I allowed my past hurts and struggles to handicap me for so many years, but now it is time to let it go. All these years I was hurting in silence, not realizing that what I really needed was healing. During my healing process, I learned that I had to minister to the pain behind the sin! I tell you my story because by some chance it might just help you. It is time to heal and move on with the life that God has planned for you! I want all my readers to know that this book is not to male bash or compare or contrast anyone else's relationships. I do share some very personal experiences with you, only to keep it real with you and show you that if by some chance you have experienced domestic violence on this magnitude or a greater magnitude, healing is still available. I know that this information will be beneficial to you in your journey to recovery. All the names have been changed, because I am not trying to connect anyone to my story. I want to say that I have forgiven "Marcus." The forgiveness was not done as a favor to him or as a gesture to man. I released him, because I could not fully have and enjoy my life while holding grudges and unforgiveness in my heart. My command is this: Love each other as I have loved you (John 15:12). We cannot allow past hurts and past struggles to hinder us from reaching our full potential. "I will not forget my past, I understand my present, but I am focusing on my future." Come and celebrate life with me!

Chapter 2

LIVING IN MY PAST

I remember the night that I woke up from another hot and sweaty dream. There was an unexplainable fear haunting me in my sleep. I tried to bury this in the pits of my mind, but at night, in my dreams it would stir itself back up and it had an overwhelming presence. I tossed and I turned. I sat up in my bed and I noticed that my nightshirt was soaked and my heart was beating fast. My mouth was dry and my eyes were filled with tears. I was crying so hard, but I couldn't remember why. It had gotten to a point that I could not distinguish dreams from reality. I had to look around the bedroom just to remember where I was. I know that this experience was real. I know that he is real and I am still dealing with my past. Now, I see that my past is actually dealing with me and more importantly I know that I should let it go. In fact, I know that I must let it go.

I tried to move on with my life, working hard each day to look decent and not damaged. I wanted to look blessed and not as miserable as I really felt. I tried to act full, but I was running on empty. My existence felt so unfulfilled, because I longed for a life filled with some peace and a little joy. Each day, I fought back the tears with a smile on my face. The outside was always together. My hair was together and my nails were always manicured. I always coordinated my accessories well with my attire. You see my glory, but you don't know my story. This make up was just a cover up. This glamour girl appearance brought me no comfort and provided me with no peace. For years I had been working over time fixing up the outside, but the inside was where all the work needed to be done. I dressed up my fears with jewelry and a smile. But when I was alone, I was scared to go to sleep at night, fearful of the memories that waited for me. On the outside, you can see that I am a woman of style and virtue, but on the inside I am mentally fading away. I continually asked myself…"How do I let go and forgive him for what he did to me?" "How do I forgive myself for allowing this to happen, and how do I forget the pain and the abuse?" "How do I let go of the memory of being abused and overcome this frustration?"

When I close my eyes I see his face, my nose twitches from the scent of his cologne.

I can still hear his voice, telling me over and over that he will kill me if I ever leave!

"If I can't have you no one else can?"

I wanted so much to forget those things that were behind me, so that I could move forward, and press toward the goals that God had for me. I wanted even more to forgive. I knew that I had to forgive him, but I was still so afraid of him? I struggled with these mixed feelings and unsettled emotions. Sometimes we think that if we avoid unresolved issues, that they would just disappear, but emotionally you remain disturbed and stressed. Somehow, I managed to teach myself how to suppress the pain. For so many years, I operated in this manner and the unforgiveness started to show up in my dreams. This unforgiveness in my heart began to hinder me mentally and physically and affect my values and my beliefs.

I had become withdrawn from others and I never talked about this abuse to anyone. What was there to talk about? This relationship was so many years ago and there are so many miles between us. But, at night, when I closed my eyes I relived the abuse and he was still there. How strange it is, 10 years later, I am still taunted by the memories of my past. I am now married with children, but this tormenting experience weighed on me daily. This man is no longer part of my life and is now in prison, on charges not even related to our past relationship. Nevertheless at night, in my dreams, I can still feel his presence. My mind was in constant turmoil trying to figure out how to overcome the dilemma of my past. In my sleep, where I am supposed to get rest and be refreshed, I became helpless and worthless. "Why did I fear him so?" My greatest fear was that he would look for me. He would find me and he would destroy me. These feelings were a result of what he had told me so many times, so many years ago. I did finally leave him, well physically I left him 10 years ago, but mentally I was still involved with wounds from my past. I was tortured by the memories and the nightmares. In these nightmares, I saw his face and I felt his presence. In every nightmare, he finds me and he repeats to me those same threats that he made 10 years ago. He tells me that this time, he will kill me! These nightmares, they felt so real and these threats became my reality. I can still remember the night that he took me away into the dark!

My Story

I clearly remember how that night started…….

Me and Marcus had come home for the weekend, as we often did. We would enjoy going out to the clubs. This weekend, we had decided not to go out and just stay in. When we got to Arkansas, we went to my sister Lisa's house. I noticed how he was flipping through his cell phone, checking missed calls, and voicemails. We had just got in town and had only been there for about an hour before he was trying to hit the streets. "I'm stepping out for a few hours", Marcus stated. I didn't respond, because I knew we had decided to stay in. Somehow he made sure that I wasn't interested in going out, yet he decided that he would go ahead and leave without me. I already knew his game. This was not the first time he had tried this one on me. He walked over to the couch, where I was sitting and started to kiss on me. I completely ignored him, because he somehow thought that this would help to ease the tension in the room. Of course, he knew that I was mad because he was about to leave, but I was tired and I didn't feel like the argument. He had already made sure that he had spent the entire day with me, which would give him an excuse to have an evening alone. Because of his desire to control, he always kept me close and under him. He made sure I had nothing else going on besides him and at the same time not wanting me to know that he had something else going on other than me. Of course, I had no proof, because I had never actually caught him doing anything unfaithful, because quite frankly we were always together. He took care of everything, just to make sure I was satisfied, which left little for me to complain about. If I wanted to go to a movie, it was done. If I wanted to go out to eat, it was a done deal. If it meant, buying me jewelry, clothes, food, VIP at the club, done! He liked to entertain, so he would buy drinks for everyone, just to show off and make himself look important. I still didn't trust him, but I tried to believe that he was true to me and to our relationship. He would typically tell me one thing and I would believe it, hanging on to his every word, as he told me that I was his one and only girl. The buzz in the streets was totally opposite of what I perceived and I was quick to defend him, even until the end. He would of course always deny any and all accusations, so in my mind my relationship was good. I could only see one side of the story and that was his side.

It was now midnight and there was no excuse for him to leave the house this late. When I started to question him, he got upset and told me to never question him. I remember standing there with my mouth open and as I was about to respond, he just turned and went out the door. I was in the middle of my sentence. I was so hot! I could not believe that he had just walked out the door, because I was not finished talking to him. I could feel a lump rise in my throat and I started screaming! I started ranting and raving telling Lisa that I was tired of this mess. I was mad and hurt all at the same time. I was mad because he left without considering my feelings and I was hurt because he didn't even care how I felt. I could never figure out why every time he wanted to go out; he somehow found something to argue with me about. I knew that this was just a ploy to blame me as his reason for leaving. I wanted it to be different. I wanted this relationship to work, so I continued to tell myself that same lame game.... "As long as he came home, I wouldn't trip." Yeah right, how simple could I be? I still tried to hold on. I was trying to make a relationship work that was doomed from the start. I learned the hard way that there was nothing worse than trying to make a man stay that was ready to go; besides there was nothing there to hold on to. He gave selfishly, as a way to make himself feel in control. He would give graciously with his right hand, while thoughtlessly taking at the same time with his left. This was part of his game. I believe that his mission was to seek full control of me and this relationship both physically & mentally. He always expected me to do exactly what he said and when he said to do it. If things did not play out like he expected, he would play the mad role until he got what he wanted. He would often flip the script on me and have me to think that all this chaos was actually my fault. I use to try and figure out what it was that I was doing wrong. I appreciated everything he did for me and I frequently let him know that. I usually agreed with him, just to avoid the conflict. There were other times when he would just leave the house to justify his childish behaviors and all the time I continued to make excuses for him and wished so hard that it would be different.

 I looked over at Lisa and she had a very worried look on her face. She told me to sit down and said we needed to talk. I was not in the mood for another one of her sermons, but I sat down with her and we began to have one of those love hate conversations. She talked to me about the importance of being in full control of yourself and your surroundings. I knew that I was just chasing my feelings, which had never proven to be beneficial for me. I didn't realize that being in full control of me and my surroundings meant just that, I only controlled myself! I could not control what Marcus did or where he wanted to go. I wanted to believe that if I told him not to go or if I got mad enough he would stay, and yes sometimes this ploy did work, but for the most part he decided when and where he would go. I had to realize that I had full control of myself and my reactions only. I was now reacting out of emotions and not responding to the situation appropriately. I should have been more in control of myself and my feelings, thinking more rationally about my situation, *love is blind*, is what Lisa told me. I was not sure why I called this thing we had love, but we were definitely blind in this relationship! The delusion of this love was meaningless and I was chasing after the wind. I told Lisa how this constant worry and pressure was affecting my studies and causing stress that I did not need. Lately, I was easily distracted and I could not stay focused on my assignments. I was having severe mood swings. I would be happy in class one minute and the next second I would get angry for no apparent reason. I had started missing class because I was too tired to get up. When I did go, I was easily agitated and didn't want to be there or talk to anyone. These episodes had me tripping out and I couldn't sleep or eat. When I didn't go to class and I had no appetite for food, I would just supplement this with other activities, to help me deal with the unwanted thoughts and current stressors. I was suppressing my feelings and hiding the abuse. I thought that I knew what love was, but I was sadly mistaken. My definition of love was so warped that I truly believed that what we had was real. I didn't know the pureness and the gentleness of love. I wanted to be loved so badly, that I stayed in this relationship. I wanted this love and I latched on to it. I held on to this perception, while sacrificing my self-esteem and my self worth. I excused the abusive behaviors and degrading remarks. All the signs were there. I saw the red flags and they were screaming WARNING to my soul! I saw these signs, but I usually turned my focus to something else, because in my mind I didn't want to understand it and my heart couldn't comprehend it. This set up for love, set me back from learning. The signs were there in the beginning. I just chose to ignore them. I ignored the manipulation and the insulting comments. Sometimes he would act jealous of my friends and family. He often blamed me for his problems and his bad moods. He wound reverse the situation, and make me feel like I was the source of the disorder in the relationship. He played innocent, and told me that I was the one who was too controlling, and that he was hurt and insulted by my actions. But, as soon as I defended myself, he would quickly get mad. These power plays were used to make me feel guilty for something he had done, which was usually followed by accusations of me doing things I hadn't even thought of doing. He would always do just enough to test the waters. He tried me many times just to see what he could get away with. He spent just enough time with me to make up for the mess up he had already made. I think I loved the thought of just having a man, more than the man himself. I have seen many women who sacrifice so much, just to say "I got a man." I too, sacrificed a lot and I loved hard, but he was not loving me back. I gave, but he was constantly taking. I gave my heart, my time, and my love, but he wasn't giving back! I was loosing myself in him. I was loosing my identity, my self-esteem, and my confidence, all in the name of LOVE!!! I was usually surrounded by him and his friends. I tried to invite him to gatherings with me and some of my friends, but he usually found a way to not go, because he said that he was not comfortable being around me and my college friends, and that I usually ignored him when I was with my friends. I wanted to accommodate him and do what made him comfortable, so I continued to hang out with him and his friends. I was allowing him to tell me what clothes to wear, how to wear my hair, and where I could and could not go. I was more focused on him and his needs that I usually neglected myself and my own needs.

I knew that Marcus loved the hype of the street life. He was infatuated with the lights, the cameras, and the action that came with this type of lifestyle. I think that in the streets is where he felt his greatest joy. This was his lifestyle and I knew it, and I still never figured out why I accepted it! I went in to this relationship knowing that he had a criminal history and a street mentality, but I continued because I liked him. I liked the undivided attention he gave and the material means of support that he provided. There was an awkward sense of hope that he would change and if I stayed around I would be the one to change him. I stayed around, but I could not compete with the street life!

I had these thoughts and I was trying to explain all of this to Lisa, but before I knew it I was mad all over again. I began yelling and telling her that the only reason I put up with him was because I felt sorry for him. I had sympathized with his lifestyle, and I tried to justify the meaning behind his criminal behaviors. I heard myself telling her, that there were no jobs in the economy for a black man, with no degree and nobody would hire a convicted felon, so he did what he had to do to make some money. I was ignorantly repeating what he had told me so many times and I guess I had started to believe that foolishness also. I believed it, because I wanted to support him, even through the hard times. I wanted to believe that this would be a temporary lifestyle for him, at least until he could find a job and make a better life for himself and for us, but loving him out of sympathy and guilt did not benefit me at all. I don't know why I did not realize then, that his life or his choices had nothing to do with me. He was content with this life and had no intentions on changing his situation to satisfy me. I'm not sure why I was so obligated to continue in a relationship that continuously drained me. His juvenile behavior was becoming a routine and I was ready to end this charade tonight. I had made up my mind that I was tired of all this confusion and I told Lisa that I was going to break up with him and that there was no reason for him to ever come back knocking at my door. I was tired of trying so hard to make this so called relationship work. I kept asking myself why I put up with him and all his drama and I somehow came up with the same answer. *I love him. I think!*

I remember standing in the middle of the kitchen, with one hand on my hip, trying to figure out how I would break up with him. In my frustration, I knew that I could just pack up my stuff and go back to campus, but did I really want to go or was I just mad for that moment. I heard somebody at the door, but I was so consumed in my thoughts that I ignored the knocking. I sat down at the table to try and gather my thoughts, but the knocking got so loud, that I couldn't even think. I looked around, and Lisa was no longer in the room to go and get the door. "Who's knocking?" I yelled, irritated because it was late and I didn't feel like being bothered. As I started walking towards the door, the knock got even louder and I became more frustrated. When I opened the door, there he stood! To my surprise, it was Marcus. I was shocked because it was too early for him to be back. He stood there with a smirk on his face. Before I could open my mouth, he grabbed me by the neck, lifted me off the floor and threw me across the room into the other side of the wall. I was so scared because this was the first time he actually attacked me. He started yelling and cussing so loud that I could hardly hear my screams over his yelling. He stood over me with one hand in fist and dared me to repeat what I had just said. I went blank for a moment, because surely he didn't hear the conversation that I just had with Lisa. He said again, "What was that you just said about me and how sorry you felt for me?" I still acted like I didn't know what he was talking about and I told him just that. "I don't know what you're talking about." I began to grasp for breath as I tried to get up off the floor. I remember looking up at him. His eyes were different, his breathing was different and he was acting irrationally. I felt a sense of fear rise up in my throat, as he began to tell me that he was at the door and had heard everything I just said about him. I knew then, that this was not going to turn out good. I looked over and Lisa was standing by the table, our eyes met with panic. I immediately jumped up and ran out the room towards the door. I ran because I knew that it was about to be some trouble. I saw Lisa, as she tried to reach out and stop Marcus from coming after me, but he pushed her down to the floor and took off behind me. I ran out the door, to the neighbor's house. I was screaming for help and hoping that someone would let me in, but no one would answer their door. I continued to run, as I felt a sense of fear move through my bones. Marcus was a big guy, standing at about six three, two hundred fifty pounds, so the thought of him hitting me again scared me speechless. I knew how controlling he was and that he liked to be in charge of every thing and every body, so I ran because I didn't need for this to escalate any further. I remember, the chase like it was yesterday. I ran across the street and back. I ran around the house and back. But no one would help me! I knew that he was really mad because of what I had said, but even madder because I had embarrassed him. I ran to another door, but still no one opened the door. I knew that these neighbors surely thought I was crazy. And they were not crazy enough to let me in. Think about it, it was the middle of the night. "Would you open up your door?" I was so scared because no one would open up their doors to help me. It was about 1:30 am, so no one in their right mind would open up the door for a total stranger. At this point, I just wanted anybody to rescue me from this chase. I sure wished they had, but they did not. I just started praying, as I kept running and crying, thinking that this man was going to kill me! I had these thoughts, because he had already told me over and over what he would do to me if I ever even thought about leaving him. I looked back and I saw him getting closer. I ran straight for the street, through a wooded area, with no shoes on. The faster I ran, the more horrific this thing started to feel. I was trying hard to get to the road on the other side, but I could feel him getting closer. He was so close that I could feel his hot breath on my neck; he was too close to me! He was screaming at me and told me to stop or he would stab me in the back. I wasn't sure if he had a knife in his hand or not and I didn't want to take any chances, so I stopped. *"If he did have a knife, would he really stab me?"* I didn't even think he would be this mad, just because I wanted to break up with him! I ran from him in the hopes of getting away or finding some help, but the seclusion and the distance from everyone else decreased my hope for help and my chance for survival. As soon as I stopped, he knocked me down to the ground. I fell down to the ground and he began to kick me! Yes, he was kicking me like I was his enemy. I guess what I had said really did make him mad. "What did I say that set him off like this?" "What did I do to make him so mad?" He was infuriated and in a deep dark rage. The first blow to my head vibrated my entire body. I remember him hitting me, as I laid there regretting everything I had just said. I can still see that closed hand fist coming towards my face. I closed my eyes praying that this would soon end, but when I opened my eyes he was still standing over me. I tried to get up, but I was instantly slapped back down to the ground. The ground was so cold and through the thickness of the dark, I could still see the look he had in his eyes. His eyes were bitter and empty, like he was in a rage and had no control over himself. He looked like he was possessed by some evil force, and I felt powerless. I can still hear his voice cursing me and telling me that he would kill me. "I will kill you before I let you leave me, he said and I dare you to try and leave now." "Do you still want to leave me?" I didn't say a word. "I guess I should feel sorry for you now, but I don't", he said. I sat there in silence and wondered if this was the end for me and if he would really kill me. He continued to ramble on, telling me that he had been to prison before and that he didn't care if he went back, especially for killing me. He said that I always thought I was better than him just because I was in college, and that I was nothing without him. He then snatched me up, by my hair and dragged me slowly to the edge of the road. I can still taste the dirt and blood in my mouth. I can feel the scratches from the rocks on my back and the burning sensation I had in my eyes. I saw a light down the road. It was dim, but I was glad to see any kind of light. The light was from a red truck and it started to slow down as it came closer to us. I just knew that this nightmare was over, as Marcus tried to stop the truck for us to get a ride. The guy pulled over, and I was nervous as he forced me to get in! I wanted to scream for help, but when I opened my mouth nothing came out. I guess it was one of his boys, because he started having a casual conversation with him like nothing was wrong. I was crying, but it was so low that I could barely hear the whimpers myself. I actually had the nerves to be embarrassed for what he had just done to me. I remember all three of us sitting tightly, in the front of this red pick up truck, and I was in the middle of him and the driver. I was pinching the driver, hoping that he would help me and praying that he would do or say something. At this point anything would have been helpful, but he completely ignored me. I could not believe this; the driver didn't say a word. Here I was hoping for a little sympathy, but I didn't have any luck. I know that the driver saw my bruised face and my torn clothes. He knew exactly what was going on, but I think that he was more afraid of Marcus than I was. I was in so much pain and I could feel the blood running down the side of my face. My jaw hurt, my head hurt, but most of all my feelings were hurt. I blamed myself, because I had said all those hurtful things about him. It had been a long night and I was tired. I just wanted this night to be over with. I sat there staring out the window. There I was, in that truck with tears in my eyes and regret in my heart. "How did I let it get to this?" I looked out the window and it seemed like we were the only vehicle on the road and just for a brief moment, it seemed like my world had stopped. I still could not believe that after all that just happened, I actually laid my head on his shoulder and went to sleep!

*Save me, O God, for the waters have come up to my neck.
I sink in the miry depths, where there is no foothold. I
have come into the deep waters; the floods engulf me.
I am worn out calling for help; my throat is
parched. My eyes fail, looking for my God.
Those who hate me without reason outnumber the hairs of
my head; many are my enemies without cause, those who seek
to destroy me. I am forced to restore what I did not steal.
You know my folly, O God; my guilt is not hidden from you.
May those who hope in you not be disgraced because of
me, O Lord, the LORD Almighty; may those who seek you
not be put to shame because of me, O God of Israel.
For I endure scorn for your sake, and shame covers my face.
I am a stranger to my brothers, an alien to my own
mother's sons; for zeal for your house consumes me, and
the insults of those who insult you fall on me.
When I weep and fast, I must endure scorn; when I
put on sackcloth, people make sport of me.
Those who sit at the gate mock me, and I
am the song of the drunkards.
But I pray to you, O LORD, in the time of your favor; in your
great love, O God, answer me with your sure salvation.
Rescue me from the mire, do not let me sink; deliver me
from those who hate me, from the deep waters.
Do not let the floodwaters engulf me or the depths
swallow me up or the pit close its mouth over me.
Answer me, O LORD, out of the goodness of your
love; in your great mercy turn to me.
Do not hide your face from your servant; answer
me quickly, for I am in trouble.
Psalm 69: 1-17*

Chapter 3

MY FRIEND:
GRACE & MERCY

I felt the truck come to a stop and I jumped up quickly. I had a headache that felt like a hangover. My head was pounding and if I could have, I would have taken a whole bottle of Tylenol. We pulled up in front of a house that I recognized. At first, things were a little blurry, but I knew that we were at one of his brother's rental homes. I thought that this night was over and I really needed to lie down. I wasn't even trying to leave. I didn't have on any shoes and I was too tired to run. "Where would I run to?" He helped me out the truck and we went in to the house. We walked into the living room and everybody was still up, but no one asked any questions. Marcus took me to the back of the house and opened the door to a half empty room. There was a dingy mattress on the floor, some boxes in the corner, and garbage bags, I assumed that were filled with clothes. There was an unpleasant smell and I was very annoyed, when he told me to sit down and not to say a word! I was too tired to even cry and too scared to say anything, at this point there really wasn't anything left to say. I just sat there, praying that God would help me. I knew that God would bring me out of this some way, some how. As I sat there, I could hear people talking in the other room. I tried to listen to see if I could recognize any of the voices, because I was sure they knew I was in that back room. As I listened, I heard a knock at the door! I heard a policeman's voice and then I heard scuffling and shuffling in the other room. I stood up, but I was not sure if I should open up the door, so I cracked the door and I peaked out. I couldn't see much, but I could hear voices, and then I heard a very familiar voice. It was my mamma and she was calling my name. I thought that I was hallucinating, but she called out again, and again. How did she find me? How did she know I was here? I could hear the panic in her voice, as she called my name. I felt a since of relief, because I knew that she was here to take me home. I was ready to get out of there, but just as I was going to the door, he came into the room. He looked at me and dared me to say a word. I thought that this nightmare was over, yet it was still happening. I was in the middle of the most terrifying moment of my life and I didn't know what to do. He continued to threaten me and my family in a low, whisper, which was very scary considering what I had been through with him already. Marcus told me that he would never let me leave him! I then heard footsteps in the other room; somebody opened the front door and said, "She is not here!" My heart sank and I could not believe this; this night was never going to end. "Who answered that door?" I know they saw me when we came into the house or did they really not know I was in that back room? "Why were they covering up for him?" He just stood over me, staring at me, with sweat running down his face. I closed my eyes, looked the other way and continued praying that God would save me from this man. As I sat on the cold hard floor, I prayed a bargain prayer…"God if you get me out of this one, I will not go back. If you spare my life, I will get it right and do all the right things by you." I had it all wrong, telling God what I would do if He helped me. I didn't know that He had already done everything and he was waiting on me to repent, receive, and believe in His precious promises.

 I could hear my mamma's voice. She was still outside, crying and scared. I wanted my mamma. I wanted her to help me and I needed her to hold me and tell me that everything would be alright. "What had I gotten myself into this time and how in the world was I going to get out of this one?" I heard the police knocking again. I guess Marcus figured they were not going to leave or that they were about to come in, so he ran out the back door. I was surprised to see him take off running and so traumatized that I didn't move, I just sat there. I nervously waited for someone to come through the door and tell me it was safe to go out, but no one did. I sat there, for about thirty seconds, which seemed like thirty minutes, before I realized that I could leave. I sat in thirty seconds of disbelief, not sure if it was over, but I got up and walked slowly out of the room to the front door and on to the porch. My mamma was the first face I saw and this night seemed like it had lasted a lifetime. She stretched her hands out to me, with tears in her eyes. I had no idea how bad I looked. I was just glad to be alive!

I thought about what had just happened and how disappointed my family was because I had gotten myself in a horrible situation like this. I didn't know what I could do or say to make this situation better. I just remember how my entire body hurt, but most of all my pride was hurt. My family was furious with Marcus for what he had done to me and they plotted to seek revenge. I pleaded with them to let it go, because I didn't want anyone else to get hurt. I knew they wanted to hurt him, like he had hurt me. I knew they wanted to break his bones and blacken his eyes, but I did not want them to catch a charge for my mistakes? I chose to be with Marcus and I could have just as easily chosen not to be with him. I knew that they were angry because I was in so much pain. It was very distressing for them to see me scared and bruised, but I needed them to think about the decisions they were about to make. I didn't want them to react violently and make a decision that could not be reversed, so I begged them to rethink their actions and find a quiet place and listen to that quiet still voice. There is that inner voice that tries to speak through the chaos in our lives and tells us how to handle any situation. It takes a strong person to decipher the voices of good and evil, and appreciate the spiritual covering of the Holy Spirit, as we try to understand that the battle is not ours to fight. Even in the middle of our storms, we must learn to walk away from that overwhelming response to react in the defense of protecting our family members. My family was definitely not considering the outcome of their actions and this was definitely a moment of decision making for them. They could not see that this one moment of their actions today, would definitely determine the outcome of their tomorrow.

    I have seen women in so many abusive situations, where the scars and bruises didn't last long. Some women may leave right after the fight, but a day or two later returns to their abuser, with fresh wounds. It often takes a woman several incidents before she actually leaves her abuser for good. So, my point to you is this….What if my family or your family does venture out and seek revenge against your abuser? The retaliation that they seek on your abuser, may be severe enough that they end up in jail. Think about it, now your family member is locked up; all the while you're laid up with a love that doesn't love you back.

    When we got to the hospital, I was hesitant to go in and I was too ashamed to talk to anyone. I remember this sharp pain on the left side of my head. I began to rub my head in hopes of making it feel better, but there was nothing there. I did have braids there, but they were all gone. I guess Marcus had pulled them out when he dragged me out of the woods to the road. I sat at the hospital and tried to make sense of this nightmare. The more I tried to figure it out, the more confused I became. When I did finally go into a room, it was cold and full of bright lights. I barely remember the faces of the people in the room that night, but I do remember having to answer a lot of questions. Most of all I remember how lonely and embarrassed I felt as I laid there in a confused state. I began to question my actions as I tried to figure out what I could have done differently. I wondered where he was, but not sure why I even cared to know. The doctors wrapped my head in several bandages. I was given some pain medication, a couple of days of bed rest and I was sent home. When I got home, I couldn't sleep. The next day when I woke up, none of it seemed real and I didn't want any visitors. People were pretending to care, but mostly they were just being nosy and were not really concerned about me. His family even tried to come by to visit but I was apprehensive because I believed that they were trying to get an update for Marcus, so, I refused to see any of them. Actually, I didn't want to talk to anybody and I really wanted to be left alone. In my room, alone is where I decided to stay and get myself together, because the humiliation disturbed me deeply. "How could I face the public with all of this embarrassment?" Looking back, I see how pathetic I was. I was more concerned about what people would think or what people would say. I was totally missing the severity of this life threatening situation. Later I heard that people were saying that this incident was actually my fault! I was dumbfounded by these commentators and instigators. "How did they figure that this was my fault?" The outsiders, of course had only seen how good this man had been to me. It was my fault because he gave me money and paid some bills. Others said that maybe it was because he was funding my college tuition and had bought me a car. Wow, did they have it all wrong! He was not paying for my school, nor had he bought me a car. He bought him a car, which he put in my name. How naïve of people to put a price tag on my life and expect me to devalue myself all because a man spent a few dollars. All these things that I thought I had were not worth the price I had to pay. The price for this thing called happiness was costing me way too much. Most people on the outside looking in talked about the money that he gave me and the clothes that he bought me. He was the town drug dealer and I was the ungrateful girlfriend because he gave me whatever I wanted. He kept me in new outfits, new shoes, and hairdos. But it cost me my self-esteem, my self-confidence and almost my life!

Precious Promise:

Though I walk through the valley of the shadow of death, I will fear no evil; for thou art with me, thy rod and thy staff they comfort me. He prepares a table before me, in the presence of mine enemies; He anoints my head with oil, and my cup runs over. Surely goodness and mercy will follow me all the days of my life and I will dwell in the house of the Lord forever. Psalm 23

Chapter 4

WHY ME?

Sometimes there is no reason. Why do we allow evil desires and sinful natures to lure us to a life of chaos and confusion? "Why me?" I asked myself this question over and over again. There is no reason and no justification for any man to abuse you. I pondered this statement, as I continued to live in a life of sin, as I tried to understand why I was stuck in this life of defeat and destruction. I continued to expose myself to ridicule, mockery, and embarrassment. I knew about some of the basic Bible bullets, and about religion, but I did not have a personal relationship with God or an understanding of any biblical principles. I had heard the Word, but never had I meditated on the Word or actually applied the Word of God to my life. There were so many weapons forming against me, which were causing a lot of destruction in my life. After the attack, it seemed like my days started to go by faster and my nights began to get longer. I sat and I watched as other people around me just continued to flourish. I should have been able to pick up the pieces of my life because Marcus and I were finally over, but somehow I still felt miserable and depressed. I remember how so many people asked me so many questions....

"What did you do; Where is Marcus; did you and Marcus break up?"

Nobody seemed to be interested in WHY he did this to me.
At this point, was "why" really an important question to ask?
But the fact remained, that I still had questions of my own.
"Why did he do this?"
Sadly enough, I didn't have an answer.

So, I kept asking myself in confusion and in doubt. "Why did I do this to me, How did I allow it to get to this point, Is this normal? If he loves me, why would he hurt me?

And because I really thought that he loved me, I often wondered what I could have done differently and maybe prevented this! I continued to tell myself that maybe I should have never said those things about him. Maybe if I would have just tried to look over him, things wouldn't have went this far. I knew that he had done a lot of nice things for me and he had tried to change, but was this material gain worth me gambling with my life and loosing my self esteem and my self worth?

At first I didn't even want to press charges. As awful as this was, and as crazy as it sounds, I still was somehow concerned about him! I began to make excuses because I knew that he had already had so many problems with the law and he had been through so much. I didn't want to make things worse for him. I thought about all the good times we had and how he always tried to make me happy. I sat there with these irrational thoughts, and then I remembered that night. Yes, that night that he treated me like his enemy. I clinched my teeth as I remembered that attack. I could hear his voice so clearly. I remember each harsh word that he said to me. I remembered the evil in his eyes and I knew then that I could not allow this man to get away with what he had done to me. I couldn't believe that I was defending his cruel behaviors and actually caring about what happened to him. I still ignorantly wanted to believe that he loved me and that he never intended for it to go this far. He had hit me before, but it was never this severe. I forced myself to believe that he had been doing better. I wanted so bad to believe that he would change. I was trying to change him, when in fact I was the one who needed to change. I had made a u-turn and I was living my life upside down. This relationship had begun to change my views on relationships and matters of the heart. What was I doing and what kind of love was this? I was being too flexible in this relationship and the standards that I once had were instantly being erased and replaced. I didn't know what to expect from him anymore. I had lowered the bar of what I expected from this man and what I would take from him. I started expecting less and taking more mess from him than I should have. Suddenly, I realized that I had been taking whatever he decided to dish out.

I did finally press charges! I knew that he should pay for what he had done to me! I wanted him to be prosecuted for what he did, but I didn't want to hurt him, even though he had already brutally hurt me and caused so much turmoil in my life. I was acting out of emotions, and still somehow missed the seriousness of this situation. Marcus was charged with kidnapping and assault. This kidnapping charge was not just a crime; it was a felony, punishable for up to 3-5 years. I remember the state picking up the case and how uncomfortable I felt going from one appointment to another, answering all kinds of questions and signing all kinds of papers.

This attack came like an expected surprise! I stayed in the relationship anticipating change, but ironically I expected destruction. I was idle in my misery, as I made up excuses to stay in this relationship. I doubted myself, my capabilities, and my potential to be loved. This doubt and insecurity is very common for many women who are in abusive relationships. The conflict and denial are as common as a winter cold, so like many victims I just treated the symptoms and waited for it to run its course. I wanted this love so bad and my desire for Marcus was so strong that I looked over the small things, which ultimately turned out to be big things. I saw the elephant in the room through the entire relationship, but like most women in this situation, I wanted it to just go away. I would close my eyes and ignorantly try to wish the pain away. I was a college girl, so I thought that I was pretty smart. I wasn't stupid, but because I poured all my efforts into maintaining a relationship with Marcus, it was hindering my thinking. This so called relationship that I was trying so hard to have just was not working out like I had hoped for. I wanted to be loved so bad that I decided to live in this dreadful relationship, with the hopes of making it work. I had gotten to a point where I didn't even recognize myself. Physically I looked the same, but I was strained mentally, and drained emotionally. I looked in the mirror daily and I knew that I loved me, but I hated that person looking back at me. "Who had I become?" I was in an abusive relationship. Yes, my boyfriend beat me up, he hit me, yet I was foolish enough then to hold on. "What was I holding on to?" I was trying to hold on to him, when I should have been trying to hold on to me, my dignity, my self-esteem, and my life. At the time, I really did not know how to handle this situation, so I just dealt with it in pieces. I look back now and realize how I played Russian roulette with my life. I did what I knew to do at the time, which wasn't much. When he was happy, I too played the happy role. I knew that the thrill would eventually be gone and I prepared myself for the next role. I was so immature in so many areas of my life. Living this life from the outside in was getting harder. I'm sure some of you know that it takes a lot of time and energy to play pretend. I truly believed that Marcus and his friends were intimidated by my enrollment in higher education and others were irritated by my nonchalant attitude. I could hear the whispers whenever we entered the room, people envied my twisted lifestyle. I had gotten caught up in a lifestyle, but I had no life. I prayed for change, but whom was I praying to. I knew who God was, but I was living such a distorted lifestyle and caught up in my wicked ways, I was sure He would smite me right in the middle of my sin.

Precious Promise:

"If my people, who are called by my name, will humble themselves and pray and seek my face and turn from their wicked ways, then will I hear from heaven and will forgive their sin and will heal their land (2 Chronicles 7:13-15).

I was covered by the prayers of my family and friends. I was so captivated by this life of sin, that I had taken that covering off and I sat exposed and under attack daily. The enemy sat patiently and waited to devour me as I drowned in my iniquities. I lived comfortably in my sin, while allowing the enemy to kill my self-worth; steal my joy, and destroy my life. I know that I was living outside of God's will, but still I wondered….. "Where was my way of escape?" Truthfully, we all can agree that I was not even trying to escape! I was the drug dealer's girlfriend, he had money, he had status, and I was enjoying all of it. I only wanted a teaspoon of grace and a half-cup of mercy. Never was I trying to get a full dose of joy or peace. I prayed out of convenience and had a part time relationship with God!

Chapter 5

CHOICES

I have set before you life and death, blessings and curses. Now choose life, so that you and your children may live and that you may love the Lord your God, listen to his voice, and hold fast to him. For the Lord is your life and he will give you many years in the land he swore o give your fathers, Abraham, Isaac and Jacob. (Deuteronomy 30:11)

We all have the ability to choose, but wisdom is the main ingredient in any choice. We must understand that good judgment is important in making decisions and we must understand that every choice carries a consequence, good or bad. Today, realize that you too have a choice. You can choose to have a life of success and triumph or failure and insecurities. I made an unusual choice that night that changed my life forever. The end results of my actions were priced much more than I had planned to pay. I never thought that this choice carried such a great consequence!

How we Met

    Me and my roommate, English came home from college for the weekend. Every weekend when we came home, we faithfully went to the club. I just knew I was cute and dressed to impress, every time I stepped out. People were always happy to see us because we were known to have a good time. At this place in my life, clubbing was on the top of my to do list and I enjoyed the night life. This particular night we were in the club and English told me that this dude wanted to buy me a drink. Of course, I was cool with that. I didn't even know who she was talking about, I just accepted the offer. But when I saw the dude, I was like, no way. I knew as soon as I laid eyes on him that I should have let this guy keep his drink and his conversation. This was the first time I met Marcus, and I knew then that he had just gotten out of prison. I knew better than to get involved with a known drug dealer. I somehow got caught up in the hype. He had a lot of money and he wanted to spend some of it on me. I was in college, with no money or job, so I was willing to explore my options. I sensed then that talking to him was wrong from the beginning, but I gambled and took this chance. Marcus and I had a brief conversation that night. He appeared to be okay and he talked a good game. His conversation was interesting and convincing. I gave him my number, and of course he called! He began to call often. I started to come home more frequently just to see him. He would give me money to go to the beauty shop and to the nail shop. It was cool, but he had a woman so I wasn't trying to intrude. I didn't like dealing with men and their baby mamma drama, so I kept the relationship "business casual". I came home every weekend and he dished out the money accordingly. I began to enjoy his company, his conversation, but most of all his money. He had a girlfriend and she started calling me. She called me several times, but it was no big deal to me, because I was only home on the weekends. He was not my man, so in my ignorance, I continued to see him. At this time in my life I had a very nonchalant attitude and was only concerned about myself! I could not believe how this female was harassing me. Her man was approaching me, yet she found it necessary to try and check me and bring this unwanted drama into my world. I had no sympathy for her and I let her know that. I wasn't trying to disrupt her home, and she needed to realize that her man was calling me. She came at me with some confrontational information, but I blew it off as nothing. I was not trying to entertain her and I definitely was not going to give her any additional information. She went on to try and tell me how he wasn't any good and that he was very demanding and controlling. I listened briefly and then hung up on her. Yes, at the time she and Marcus were still together and because she was the live in girlfriend, I wasn't expecting any good news from her. I told Marcus about the harassing calls from his woman and he was very upset. He then tried to confront me by trying to tell me how to handle his woman, not realizing that I had no love for him or his sidekick. This backdoor relationship between me and Marcus had become unexpected public knowledge. Rumor was that every time the girlfriend called me, he ruffed her up a little. One girl even told me that he liked to hit his women. This wasn't important to me, because I knew that he knew better than to ever try and put his hands on me. Somehow, I thought I was exempt! I foolishly thought that I could continue to enjoy the benefits, with no strings attached. I have learned however; that there is a price to pay for everything. He continued to pursue me and had told me on several occasions that he wanted to be with me and only me. I somehow started wanting him, minus the girlfriend, but not realizing that I was sowing a seed of deceit and destruction towards myself.

Think about it, just as a farmer plants small seeds for corn and tomatoes, it is no mystery to them when they come back; there is their harvest of ripe corn and tomatoes. We too, must understand that we get exactly what we planted. And though it starts off as a small seed, with time that seed of dishonor, disobedience, and deceit will grow! I was setting myself up for failure. I interrupted somebody else's home and intruded on somebody else's life. I somehow believed that I could be happy, while all the time making someone else's life miserable. I dared to smile off someone else's frown. I was selfish and conceited and I was only concerned with my own needs! I didn't care about trespassing, as I explored territory that was off limits. Ladies, please understand that when we intrude on someone's relationship, hoping to find love we usually linger along with no direction, running into barricades and we end up on a dead end road every time.

I now see the evilness in what I did. I now know that there is no glory in rejoicing off others misery. I was young, self centered, and very foolish. It was very inconsiderate of me to intrude on the lifestyle of someone else. I was playing a thoughtless game and hoping to win. I played this game with no sympathy, no compassion, and the lack of Christ in my life. I ignorantly continued the late night phone calls with him. We started going out to dinner and I started to like him. I never intended to like him, but I was already caught up in a world where I did not belong. I had gotten comfortable in my sin and we had agreed that we would keep it real with each other. He broke it off with the girlfriend, so *I thought*, because he said that he wanted to be with me and me only. These words captured my attention, and I let my guard down. The relationship went from 0 – 100 and we began a sexual relationship. Things began to get too serious!

Chapter 6

SHACKING

The summer after school was out, I came home and we moved in together. Believe it or not, after all the drama with his girlfriend, he wanted us to live together and even worse, I did too. At the time I didn't realize how crazy this was. I was just happy to be moving in my own place with my man. He told me that if I agreed to move in with him he would pay the rent on us a house. I knew that he would fully furnish it and he would let me pick whatever I wanted, so I agreed. I was excited because he would pay all the bills. I had no worries! This sounded too good to be true. I was so happy, but I was the only one excited about this move. When I told my family that I was moving in with Marcus they just gave me this blank look. I felt like they were just jealous because I had an opportunity to get my own place. I really didn't care what they thought; I was caught up in my own world, thrilled to be getting a house with Marcus! We went to the furniture store that weekend and I enjoyed taking the day to pick and choose my furnishings and fixtures. I picked out my bedroom suite, with a matching comforter. I got a really nice living room set, with all the matching accessories. He even gave me extra money to buy some additional things for the house. I was so excited because I had never had a man to provide for me like that. I thought that because he was giving me his money, it was a sure sign that he really loved me. I knew he had some things he needed to work on, but as I overlooked his mishaps, I continued to think he would eventually change his manipulative ways. I just knew he would. He made it seem like it was all about me and I was ignorantly loving every moment of it. At the time I did not even realize that it would cost me my freedom and my independence.

I was in a nice house that was fully furnished. I was in my own house, but I was alone. Yes, alone. I thought that I would be overjoyed. I had so much to be happy about. I had some money in my pocket, a little house on the corner, and my bills were paid. I even had a man, but I was still lonely. I was lonely, scared, and somewhat depressed. (He who loves silver will not be satisfied with silver, nor he who loves abundance with gain. This also is conceit – Ecclesiastes 5:10).

From the beginning, I thought that these material possessions would make me happy. These things that I possessed actually possessed me. These things didn't comfort me and they definitely couldn't talk to me. I had locked myself into a world of false hope and wishful thinking. Marcus was never at home. I didn't have much company and I rarely went anywhere. I think it was just easier that way. It was usually easy, if I just did what I was supposed to do and let him of course do whatever he wanted to do. He now had more freedom to come and go as he pleased and he had me in a place where he knew where I was at all times. I thought he was a good man to have around. I thought I enjoyed his company and I made myself believe that I enjoyed him. When I did go somewhere, it was harder to come back to this house that I was calling home. Each day it got harder to walk in my own house. I felt like I was walking into the dark, deep into the woods. I was fearful of what waited for me or what I might see. In this walk, I sensed the fear of walking in the woods and seeing a snake! But, I continued on, hoping not to have to encounter the terrifying sight of this vicious creature. I am cautious with which direction I will go and I watched every step, because if I stepped on a snake, it might just bite me, which of course could be deadly. And though some of us fear snakes, there are others that have snakes for pets. These people train their snakes; they feed their snakes, but they are sure to keep these snakes in a cage. They recognize that it is still a snake and that they must be very careful when handling them. Marcus, he often reminded me of a snake! The sight of him frequently scared me. His presence normally made my stomach turn, but I wanted to keep him. I wanted to care for him and I tried to be nice to him, but he would always remind me that he was still a snake. His actions were sometimes vicious and unexplainable. As careful as I tried to be, I had been bitten. This poisonous bite caused my heart to swell; it spread quickly and made me feel nauseous, as I longed for this love that I could never understand.

I think that Marcus used me to validate his manhood. I believe that he truly hated himself, so he tried to strip me of my dignity and self-worth to make himself feel better. He fed off my success and my dreams. He would make me and my education the topic of all his conversations, not to boast on me, but as an avenue to show off and make himself look good. As ridiculous as it sounds to me now, I remember standing there right beside him, just as proud and foolish as ever. He made me miserable because he was miserable. I wanted him to love me, but now that I think about it, I don't even think he liked me! He constantly made me feel small, so he could look tall. Maybe I wasn't scared of him; I was just scared of what he was capable of doing to me. This entire relationship was built on lust and lies. All the good that he did was for his own selfish fulfillment. He thought he was giving, but actually he was taking. I thought loving him was the right thing to do, but it was not an easy thing for me to do. I wanted to love him so bad, but I had to love everything that he was and everything he had been. I didn't want to fail at this relationship, and I actually doubted my ability to succeed at a real loving relationship. I ignored all the signs. I just blew it off like it was nothing. I ignored all these things because I was afraid if I said something, I would run him away. I could not and I would not loose the only man that I thought had ever loved me. I refused to accept that I was following this love, like a pig going to the slaughter. I was young and lacked judgment and wisdom. I never took out the time to get to know him. I did not know what his interests were or his goals in life. I never asked him about his past relationships. I just allowed him to lure me with his persuasive words and smooth conversation. I listened, as he reassured me that everything would be just fine and I made a sexual commitment that caused me to live deeper in shame and disgust. How many times do we allow our flesh to deceive us? Many times our eyes see how good he looks, our ears are instantly filled with broken promises of love, and our mind receives the lies as truth. How many women defy themselves by getting sexually involved with an abuser and often feel that they are past the point of no return!

I made his misery my misery. I found myself explaining his behaviors to others and often times trying to also explain my behavior, but no one ever understood. No one ever understands, because they are all on the outside looking in. Have you ever noticed how people judge you by the smile on your face and the clothes on your back? They do not even know that you are really trying to cover up the pain and hold back the tears. I felt that I could not tell anyone what was going on in my world. And I was afraid to say anything to him, in fear of what he might do to me, so I held on. But, why was I holding on? I wasn't married to him and we didn't have any kids or financial obligations. I still remained true to him. I was being faithful. I was being loyal. I wanted to help him and I wanted to change him. I was so busy thinking about changing him; I overlooked the drastic changes that were happening to me.

I was so caught up in this abnormal relationship, that I didn't even notice how he started to come home later and later. Marcus's lifestyle was changing rapidly and we started to have constant traffic during the day. Of course this bothered me, but I never said anything. I think what upset me most, was seeing people that I knew coming to get a fix. It was mind boggling to see these people with good jobs and good reputations hooked! I could not believe that they were hooked on drugs so tough! I was trying to figure out how this addiction had them sacrificing their family, their jobs, and spending their whole paychecks! I never said a word and I had to be invisible. I had to see nothing, hear nothing, and never ever say nothing. He was the supplier and I was the ungrateful girlfriend. I knew that this was not the life for me, but I thank God that I did not get caught up in this lifestyle. I thank God that I was still somehow covered in the middle of all this illegal activity.

The situation was moving at a faster pace and I was getting nervous. I took a deep breath and I decided to question him. I began to express my concerns, but he slapped me so hard, I think I literally saw stars. He was furious and said that I dared not to ever question him again. He told me that he was a grown man and I had no right to question what he did and that I knew how the game was played before I decided to join the team. He then said that he paid the bills, took good care of me, and I should be satisfied with that. I thought to myself "satisfied," it was only a thought and I didn't say another word! There was a long, loud, moment of silence, as he turned and walked out the room. I heard the back door slam and the car speeding down the street. I sat down on the edge of the bed and realized that this was just another reason for him to leave me at home, and another reason for me to be alone. I picked up the phone and attempted to dial, but I quickly put it back down. I could call my friends or my family, but I was too embarrassed to tell anyone. I laid down for a moment and just pretended that it would be okay. I was mixed up in my own sadistic life. I sat alone in my dark hole and tried to drown my misery away. I remember when the phone rang, it startled me. It was my mother. I told her how great things were, fighting back tears, and that I was tired and would call her tomorrow. I had become more isolated from my family and friends and more dependent on him. I would just lie awake many nights crying and wishing that my relationship would get better. The tears increased as my love for myself decreased. In my darkest hour I kneeled down by my bedside, on my knees, eyes full of tears and heart full of regret.

Now, I lay me down to sleep
I pray the Lord my soul to keep.
The angels watch me through the night
and keep me til the morning light. Amen

Even then living in my sin, in my darkness, I knew that God was my night light. For You, O Lord, are my Lamp, the Lord lightens my darkness (2 Samuel 22:29).

I thought that I had it all together. I was grown and out on my own. I was playing house and trying to handle grown folks business. I had gotten to a point where I did not want to listen to anyone. "This is my life and I would make my own decisions." I resented anyone that tried to tell me how to live my life or handle my relationship. I didn't realize that I needed guidance and that my friends and family were trying to protect me. I continued to suffer through this alone, thinking that I could fix it, hoping that it would get better, but knowing that I was in love with a love that didn't love me! This rocky road was a flavor that I was somehow getting use to. I was sinking in my own pain and drama. I sat there in the dark and did what I did most nights. I cried myself to sleep.

I knew that I was not supposed to be living like this. I woke up the next morning about 3:30 am and there he was, just standing over me. I don't know how long he had been there, but he was just staring at me. I was so startled, but I didn't say a word and he just stood there like nothing was wrong. This was too much for me. This was yet another scary and dangerous episode, but I didn't ask him any questions. I just sat straight up in the bed and looked at him as he got in the bed like everything was normal. This thing was getting worse by the day! This relationship was poisonous and very hazardous to my health. Things had gotten so crazy and to make matters worse, I wanted to get pregnant. I didn't really want to have a baby; I just wanted to have Marcus. I wanted him to stop hitting me and just love me, so I figured that if I got pregnant the abuse would stop and he would love me more. I pretended to be pregnant! I knew that this would make him happy and he would stop hitting on me! This charade lasted briefly and the newness of that news wore off quickly. It wasn't long before he started right back up with his evil ways and abusive behaviors. I told him I had a miscarriage and with the way he was tossing me around, it wasn't hard for him to believe. This thing was getting the best of me. I never thought I would be here. Looking back at this situation, getting out may appear to some to be an easy thing to do. It sure would have been the smart thing to do. I know that I should have gotten out sooner, but back then, getting out was hard for me. It was so hard because I thought I was in love. I somehow thought that this was love! I was standing at the door of fear and on the other side was my freedom. I remember thinking of ways to leave this relationship unharmed. As I reflect on the doorway to my freedom, it seemed to be unlocked and all I had to do was open it up and walk right through. I reflect on this and I take a mental attempt to twist the knob. I twist it and I turn it, until I realize that I am locked in from the inside. Yes, locked in my own private hell and I can't get out. I am suffocating from these lies and drowning in my own depression. I am drowning in despair, until I finally realized that the door to my freedom is actually unlocked. As I come up for a breath out of my depression and despair, I see the knob right at my fingertips. I look at it for a long time, I think about how I can truly make a difference in this relationship if I stay. I reach over to the knob, taking a step towards my freedom, but then, I turn and walk away!

I strolled right back into this situation feeling helpless and alone, trying to remember my life before this man. I strained my brain trying to think about our few good days. I continued on with this relationship, living in bondage. I walked hopelessly around in circles of misery and mayhem. I stayed in this relationship because I was afraid to leave. I was afraid of life without him. I know how stupid this may seem, but at the time, this was my reality. I wished that I could magically be removed from this mess I was in. I wanted these feelings to be taken away and these unwanted desires to be ripped away, but I knew in my heart that I had to give it up. I had to give him up! I remember looking at him and wondering what was wrong with him, but I quietly asked myself, what was wrong with me!

Chapter 7

NO MORE PRETENDING

He loves me. He loves me not. He loves me. He loves me NOT.......
I continued to call this love, but it looked so different from that typical TV type of love. I wanted that boy meets girl; we fall in love and live happily ever after. Okay, even with all the problems and issues, I still believed in him. I still believed in us. He could possibly change and we would then be able to live that happily ever after. I was trying so hard to enhance this romance, but I had to realize that there was no happily ever after to my story. My fairytale romance was turning into a horror film and I was the main character.

I was so nervous the day I decided to leave, but I was more afraid of what else would happen to me if I stayed. I was tired of pretending to be happy and there was just nothing else to try and work out. I made up my mind that I had taken enough. I had to get myself out of this mess, before he killed me, I killed me, or I killed him. It was a chilly Saturday night and I knew that he would be out late. I packed up a few personal items and headed out the door. I left most of my things at the house. I didn't want any of it and I sure didn't want anything that reminded me of him. I certainly didn't want to give him the pleasure of identifying his stuff and what he had paid for. Usually, when we had one of these moments and he got mad, he would quickly remind me of what he had paid for. This was not the first time I had left him. I had tried many times before to leave him, hoping to end this chaotic relationship. My intentions each time was to run far away from all these problems, yet these unresolved issues continued to haunt me! I was trying to run away from it all, but somehow it was still there. No matter which way I turned, I was still in a state of confusion. I was still lonely. I was still scared and I still had mixed feelings for Marcus.

I wasn't sure how he would react, when he came home and I was gone, but I left anyway. My cousin lived right around the corner, so I would just go to her house. I walked quickly up the street, hoping I could make it around the corner before he came home. As soon as I turned the corner, I saw bright, flashing headlights. I felt my heart drop and it was like I could hear his motor running and his tires squealing. I could not believe he was already coming home. He never came home this early. I was shocked to see him and my heart began to beat so fast. I could not move. He stopped the car in the middle of the road, jumped out the car and started yelling at me. "Where are you going this time of night?" I told him that I was scared and I decided to go up the street to Stacy's house. I had my bags in my hand, so he knew that I was lying. He smacked me to the ground and as I tried to get up, he slapped me down again. A car was coming up the road, so he had to get in his car to move it out of the way. As soon as he got in, I took off running up the road. I made it to Stacey's house and started beating on her window. She looked out the window and saw it was me; she quickly came to the door. As soon as she opened the door I went in and locked the door as fast as I could. We stood there looking out the window and we saw Marcus's car driving by. She looked at me, but she didn't ask any questions, she already knew the story. I just went to the other room. I tossed and turned all night and I could not go to sleep. I left Stacey's house early the next morning, with little sleep. I went back to my mamma's house and tried to finally get some real rest. I slept most of the day. I woke up about 2:00pm and I had 25 missed calls. As, I was checking the messages, most of them were from him and he was calling again. I answered anxiously, wanting to talk to him, just to hear what he had to say. He began to ask me questions about my day, who I was with, where did I go, and what did I do? I instantly started to explain and told him I had to go to the laundry mat because somebody had stolen some of my clothes off the clothesline. He quickly responded to let me know that he had taken my stuff. I was shocked, but not really. I kind of expected some childish prank like this from him. He said that he had paid for them and wanted them back. I somehow thought that this was funny and very ridiculous. He told me that I could come and get them from him. I responded angrily and told him that he could keep that stuff and get a life!

As I hung up the phone, I felt a sense of relief. It had gotten easier for me to leave, but I was beginning to feel lonely. Yes, I did feel alone and I did not like this feeling. I started to rationalize why these things were happening to me. I was trying to figure out what I should have done differently or how I could make things work out better. I knew that I had made the right decision to leave, but the loneliness and anxiousness caused unrealistic thoughts. I was listening to his broken promises and I started to tell myself that if I took him back this time, he would change. I knew that it would be better the next time around, because this is what he told me. I talked to him a lot on the phone, because I had no one to talk to that would understand my feelings! I tried to talk to family and some friends, but they were so harsh and judgmental. No one seemed to be concerned about how I felt. No one tried to understand my loneliness and my hurt. When I tried to talk to them, they just wanted to tell me what to do or what they would do. They would bash Marcus and say so many ugly things about him, which only made me feel that I was obligated to defend him. I now realize that their forward approach was only because they loved me and was concerned for my safety. Marcus and I had broken it off and I felt a sense of relief and despair all at the same time. I was relieved because I finally mustarded up the strength to leave him. As soon as I thought I was getting over him he started calling more frequently. At first I would let the phone ring and refuse to answer, afraid that I may actually believe his lies. As the days passed I didn't have the courage to ignore his calls. I felt like I was addicted to this fascination of love. I couldn't understand why I continued to long for him. I continued to think about him and I continued to want him. I wanted his touch, his smell, and his conversation. Through my own ignorance I thought that he would change and I continued to hold on. I contemplated on going back and I tried to fight the urge to return to him. I ignored all the bad times, and mentally erased all the mistreatment and focused on the few good times we had. I wanted this relationship to work for all the wrong reasons. The phone calls increased and the more I talked to him, the more I wanted him back in my life. I left him because I knew then that the relationship was toxic, yet here I was plotting and planning on going back! I was walking back into a door that said "Do Not Enter" and playing with fire, hoping not to get burned!

"I'm sorry," this is what he said to me.

This apology confused me because I knew that it was a ploy just to get him back in the door. 'I'm not even sure what he was sorry for?" "What does I'm sorry even mean?" He said it, with so much sincerity, and he talked to me like he had amnesia and had forgotten about all the fighting and the cussing. "Baby, give me one more chance." I was fighting a loosing battle, and listening to his smooth talk as he told me everything that I wanted to hear. It disturbed me even the more because not only did I listened to him, I also accepted it. How many of you too, have accepted all of the lies and the scheming ways, just because it somehow comforts you in your quest for success in a relationship that you know is contaminated? You listen intensely; as he tells you everything you wanted to hear!

Unfortunately for me, he said just that.

"I'm sorry!" and "I love you!"

These are the three words that can make you or break you. These words, these three words can heal and they can hurt. These words were so comforting to the inner me in this time of loneliness. These three words gave hope to my pain and pulled strenuously on my heart. He said that he was so sorry and that he would never hit me again. I can't say that I believed any of it, I just accepted it as an excuse for me to get back with him. I was so glad to be talking to him on the phone and I listened with a big smile on my face. I listened, while he continued to feed me the same empty promises. I knew this was unacceptable, but I fell for that same game again. "How could I not go back to him?" "He had given me a house and all the things that I thought I wanted." I wanted to believe that he would change and I thought that I could change him. Man, was I ever wrong! It felt wrong. It felt so wrong, yet I wanted to make it right. I wanted to believe that he would change and that it would be different this time. He said that he loved me, yet he was the source of my pain. He said that he cared about me, yet he was the one hurting me. I made a conscious choice to go back. I knew what I was doing; I just didn't understand why I was doing it. I wanted to try this thing again, hoping for change. I did not allow adequate time for my mental wounds to heal. I was so in love and desperate for his companionship that I went right back in this relationship with fresh wounds. These self-inflicted wounds were never treated and never had time to heal. His presence was a temporary fix for what I dreadfully desired. My definition of love had been diluted with lust, lies, and sacrifices. He would go through phases when he was just so nice. I literally thought that I was on cloud nine, but like the flick of a light, his behavior could instantly be turned on and then off again.

The summer was now over and it was time for me to go back to school. English and I shared a room last semester, but this semester, she decided to move into her own apartment. She said that she was tired of the fighting and the fussing she had seen all summer and fed up with the drama between Marcus and me. She told me that she could not understand why I continued to put up with this man and his mess. She tried on several occasions to talk to me, but I didn't care to listen. She didn't understand that this was my man and I was determined to make this relationship work out. I was going to make this work because I loved Marcus. I just didn't realize how much loving him was costing me. I use to sit around and look at how happy every body else was in their relationships. All these young people, on campus were going on with their lives and enjoying each other. They were not concerned about me nor did they care if I had a man or not. I was mad because most of the people that were telling me to leave my man were still hanging on to their no good men. So of course, I didn't listen to them. I didn't care what they thought. I was doing whatever I needed to do to keep my man, no matter what the cost. I never realized that it would cost so much. I had charged so many of his faults to the game that I was going bankrupt. I was overdrawn mentally and emotionally. My heart was reading insufficient funds. I was in debt and I couldn't pay the accumulated interest. I would never be able to pay the price for this crazy type of love.

This was my last semester of college and Marcus went back to campus with me. He actually moved in my dorm room. This of course was against all policy and procedure, but I didn't care. I was on an emotional roller coaster, so I took the risk. How bad could it be? He had a copy of my class schedule and dared me to be late getting out of any of my classes. At first, I thought that this was sweet, but a bit controlling. I had no friends and he wanted to know my every move and of course I entertained him by keeping him informed. We mostly sat around the room, because we didn't have money to do much else. Marcus had gotten a car, which was in my name, for legal reasons. When he decided to get the car, I of course didn't realize the long term effects of credibility or credit score. I later, had to endure some unresolved legal issues, because of this careless decision I made.

One day we were out just riding, it was a typical day and he started tripping out on me. I don't remember why, but of course he didn't really need a reason. We pulled over and he was still flipping out accusing me of all kinds of stuff. He actually didn't hit me this time. He hit the windshield! He smashed his hand into the window so hard, that he cut his hand and cracked the window straight down the middle. He was tripping out, and there I sat like a knot on a log trying to figure him out.

I had to find some outside activities to keep me occupied and to give this relationship a break. I talked about getting a part time job, and he did not like this idea. He didn't want me to get a job because this meant I would have my own money and not have to depend on him. I never really knew how much money he had because he gave me what he wanted me to have, which of course was another way for him to be in control. I finally convinced him that I would only work a few hours a week and we could have some spending money. I filled out numerous applications and I finally got a job at Wendy's. Marcus would often come up to my job with some of his friends, eat, and hang out until I got off. He always took me to work and picked me up from work. One day I didn't see him all day. I had to get a ride to work and when I called him, he didn't answer his phone. I remember waiting on him to come and pick me up. I waited outside for thirty minutes and he did not show up, so I got a co-worker to take me home. I felt bad about having to hitch a ride and I was hesitant because I didn't want Marcus to come pick me up and I not be there. I knew that this would make him mad! How awkward was that, here I am concerned about him being mad. Not only was he late picking me up, I hadn't seen him all day. I think I was more concerned about him tripping out on me because I got a ride from somebody else and then all the excuses and accusations would start. I was not in the mood for this and I wanted to just go to my room and rest... alone. I opened up the door and he was already there. He was there waiting on me! I felt a turning in my stomach, because I knew that he was about to flip out on me. He said that he had been to my job twice and I was already gone. I knew he was lying.

Why was he even going there with me?

Before I knew it, he was choking me.

It was weird because I didn't even cry. I said nothing, closed my eyes and prepared my mind for whatever came next. I was numb and I felt nothing. At this point, I really didn't even care.

I knew I didn't do anything.

Why did I put up with this?

Where is the balance?

I had no balance in my life.

I was either real stupid or real desperate.

I now sit and reflect on how I had so many excuses, but that was then and this is now. Even now, women still have so many excuses as to why they are still sitting in an abusive relationship looking for balance. "Is there any balance between abuse and affection?"

The next day, he promised that he would never hit me again. He added some more cheap promises and pleaded that he wanted this relationship to work. He said that he didn't want to loose me, and that was why he acted out like that. I took it for what it was worth and went on about my day. That night we went out for a movie and a nice dinner. After dinner we went for a long, nice drive. We drove down to the park and we just sat there and talked. I was enjoying myself because we were finally having a nice quiet time together. It was just me, him, and the night air. The river was pretty and the moon was full. Marcus leaned over and kissed me on the cheek and then told me that if I ever left him, he would kill me. Just think, he said, I could kill you right now and nobody would ever know. Nobody would ever find you out here!

I knew that it was time for me to pack up my things and go, AGAIN! I knew that leaving would not be easy, but staying was not an option for me. I was tired of making all these sacrifices and adjustments just to be pumped up by this man and kicked down all at the same time. I didn't have the courage to face him or the strength to fight him, so I decided to call his sister, who lived in the same town. I asked her to talk to him and tell him that I wanted him to move out! I told her to tell him that I wanted him to get his stuff and leave my room or I would call the police. I was in between classes when I made the call and I wasn't sure where he was, so I stayed late after class. I left class with a group of my friends and walked across campus. I didn't go back to the dorm for a couple of days, because I knew that he would be watching me. I knew that he was crazy like that, so I had to take care of me. I missed class and work that week because I was afraid of what he might do to me, but I eventually had to go back to my room. I returned to my dorm room on a Thursday night. I had the campus security to escort me there, because I didn't know what to expect. I opened the door and to my surprise, there was nothing there! I mean absolutely, nothing! He wasn't there and nor where any of my things. He had taken all my stuff! Everything I ever owned was gone! My TV, my stereo, my clothes, my sheets off the bed and my poster pictures off the wall. Everything! I opened my dresser drawers and it looked like no one had ever lived there. My God, what was I suppose to do. I felt like I had been robbed. I knew that this was part of his game. This was his way of playing mind games with me as he always did. His manipulative behavior indicated that this was another way for him to control the situation. He had some family in town, so I knew where he would be. I knew that he had taken my stuff because he wanted me to come get it. I was so mad, but I did just that. I went to get my stuff! I called the police, so that they could meet me at the house. I remember pulling up in the driveway and he was the first face that I saw through the window. I quickly got out my car, and walked up to the door. I dreaded the confrontation that I knew I had to endure. I went into the house with the police and he was sitting there with his boys and some females watching my TV! He began to make an unpleasant scene. He was so cold and he talked to me like I had taken his stuff. At first, I didn't say a word, but then I asked him to give me my things. He didn't even acknowledge that I was standing there he just start talking to the police telling him that these were his things because he had paid for them. He looked over at me and said some very hurtful things, but I just stood there with a look of disgust on my face. I felt like my heart had been violated. My mind and heart were tangled and my emotions were strangled, as I tried to break free from the voices of my flesh. I felt like I was loosing my mind and I wanted to cut him, spit on him, slap him, anything that I could to hurt him. He did his best to belittle me. He sat there with a grin on his face, while smoking and drinking like I didn't exist. I don't know if I was hurt because he was playing with me or shame because he was embarrassing me. He playfully handed me a garbage bag with all my personal things in it. I was so humiliated that I could have just sunk right through the floor. He did not have to give me back the other stuff, because I could not prove that it was mine. Of course his homeboy lied and said that the other stuff was his, as I stood there in disbelief. I could not cry. I would not cry in front of these losers. I fought back the hot tears. It was hard, but I did not cry. I left without saying a word. I did not say one word. After all I had sacrificed and put up with, I could not believe that Marcus had the nerve to disrespect me like this. I somehow thought that I was exempt from his ridicule and his mockery and I was looking for a get out of jail free card. I had been playing with fire and I had gotten 3rd degree burns. I suffered alone because who would respond to this mess that I was in "Again!" I didn't think I deserved any sympathy or compassion; I just became unresponsive to this dead situation. "Who would understand my distorted feelings?" "Was this my fault because I continued to run back to him?" I chose this lifestyle. I chose this relationship.

I know that this was a crazy choice, but I had the power to change this situation! I knew that I needed to get myself together and continue on with my life. I continued to push my way through school and I continued to go to work almost every day. I cried some nights, but I smiled through most of my days. Things were good for me and I was living my life again and realizing that I could survive without a man in my life. Just when I thought I was starting back on the right track in my life, things took a turn. I wanted so bad to pledge a sorority and of course I needed some money. I was saving my checks from work, but it was hard. I had just gotten my first car and I wasn't making that much at Wendy's. He called! How foolish of me to be excited, but after 2 months, I was just happy that he had called! Yes, believe it! It was true, I was happy to hear his voice, but I was scared to death of what he was going to say next. I had a very strange feeling of excitement and fear ball up in the pit of my stomach. It was so weird how this man excited me, but scared me all at the same time. He said that he heard I needed some money and he would give it to me with no strings attached. At first I refused, but day after day I was falling for him all over again. He took care of what ever I needed him to and I started falling for this so call love again. He was waiting patiently to ruin me all over again and I helped him out by allowing him back in my life. It was my slipup, as I messed up and allowed myself to get caught up in this world of lust and lies, "Again!" When I talked to him on the phone, my thoughts were racing and my energy level was out of control. The five-minute phone calls turned to 30 minutes, and the excitement in my voice began to rise and I was falling weak to the game. Before I knew it, we were dating and making up. I was back in his trap all over again, all by choice, with no thought of the consequences. I remember how excited I was about pledging. I was finally going to be a part of something bigger than me. I also knew that this would give me a break from Marcus. I wanted to build new relationships and help to make a change in my community, so I committed to learning and educating myself about the sorority that I wanted to join. I realized that this was a very strenuous task, even for a soldier like me. I was determined to form relationships with other women, because I too wanted to promote sisterhood, service, and scholastic achievement. Even with all the chaos and confusion I had going on in my life, I still wanted to be a part of a sisterhood that promoted education and exceptional service. I was going to school, working, pledging, and trying to juggle a man. It was hard because I had to explain every thing to him. My every move was questionable. He preferred for me to have no outside interest and he wanted to dictate who my friends should or should not be. I missed a lot of the meetings and some of the activities just because it was easier if I didn't have to explain anything to him. I made it to all the mandatory meetings, but anything that was for my own fun and enjoyment I just skipped out on. I continued to play pretend as my relationship headed straight for destruction! I thought that this twisted relationship would straighten itself out, but the harder I tried to understand it, the more confused I became. I tried to logically rationalize it, because none of it was making sense to me anymore. The fact of this matter was, that this was one wild and crazy love and a very screwed up situation! But the truth is that I continued to love him and I did everything I could for him to love me back. I accepted him and his abnormal behaviors, because he provided for me and through all his rage he still offered me a false sense of security. He gave me whatever his money could buy, because this was a reflection of him. I delusionally thought of him as my hero, but who would save me from him.

It is so weird how I thought that all this stuff that he gave me was connected to love. I placed so much value on material gain and building up the outside that I was tearing down the inside. I was loosing myself in this world of sin. I was looking good on the outside, but the inside was demolishing daily. I continued to hang on to this overwhelming feeling of emotions and this crooked smile. I now think that feeling I had for all those years was just indigestion! Seriously, now that I've had a good dose of real love. I know that love is patient, love is kind. It does not envy, it does not boast, it is not proud. It is not rude, it is not self-seeking, it is not easily angered, and it keeps no record of wrongs. Love does not delight in evil but rejoices with the truth. It always protects, always trusts, always hopes, always and preserves. Love never fails (1 Corinthians 13:4-8).

I continued to hope for that patient and kind type of love. I wanted to change this uncomfortable love I was experiencing with Marcus. Never mind that, I needed to just change partners altogether. "Switch!" "When would my change come?" Yes, it was past time for me to make a dramatic change in my life and in my lifestyle. Have you been thinking about making some changes? Like me, you must understand that if change is to occur, you must of course believe that change is possible. "What are you telling yourself?"

God grant me the serenity to accept the things I cannot change
Courage to change the things I can and
Wisdom to know the difference
Reinhold Niebuh

"Greater is He that's in me than he that is in the world"
"I am fearfully and wonderfully made"
"I will trust in my God with all my strength…

I have learned that we can create our own success or failures by the words we speak over our lives and by the choices that we make. Ask yourself, "Am I setting myself up for failure?" Ladies, I have realized that when we practice responsible behaviors our outcomes are usually successful. For me, it was those irresponsible behaviors that lead to consequences that I did not want to deal with. I began to make excuses and blame everybody else for the results of my bad decision making. I did finally realize that it was very possible for me to a live more productive life once I changed those self defeating thoughts and irresponsible behaviors. I have learned the importance of accountability and how to be more tolerant with myself and others around me. I now know that if you change the way you think, it will definitely change the way you feel. You have to learn to take responsibility for the way you live your life. In order to take ownership of my life, I had to reflect back on what I did and what I allowed to happen. I listened to some crazy things, which made me have some crazy thoughts. I allowed some crazy people to influence me and I made some crazy decisions. All in all, I hold myself accountable for the choices I made! In hindsight, I see how I opened up doors to greed and selfish desires, and I allowed sinful natures to devour me. I welcomed dishonest behaviors and unhealthy practices. I let fornication, desperation, immaturity, and ignorance persuade me to a life of lies. In our little minds, we unrealistically think that fornication is okay. Well, we know that it is not okay, but we still hold on to sexual soul ties and we participate in sexual sin. It is past time that we take heed to the biblical principals and purge ourselves of old thinking, old habits, and our old ways. As you repent for your sins, allow the love of God to cover you, protect you, and minister to you.

Precious Promise:

Do not conform any longer to the pattern of this world, but be transformed by the renewing of your mind. Then you will be able to test and approve what God's will is—His good, pleasing and perfect will.
(Romans 12:2)

I was still somehow conformed to the patterns of the world. I had not yet renewed my mind and was definitely out of the will of God. I continued catering to my flesh, not recognizing at that time, that I was contaminating my emotions, my thoughts, and my actions. I ignored all the warning signs and robbed myself of happiness. This toxic relationship was causing destruction to my body both physically and mentally. My relationship with Marcus was based on an aspiration for love and a desire for material things. Right and wrong was so jumbled up that I really didn't care anymore. I allowed this man to control me with his intimidation and his manipulation. I was not being real with myself and I was not being real with God. I was advocating fornication and I chose to stay in an abusive relationship. I do not blame myself for his actions and I make no excuses for his behavior; I do however understand now that we live by the choices that we make and to every choice there is a consequence. I have learned to make better choices and I pray that you to have grasp the importance of making the right choices in your life. I know that each of us have the power to make choices, but I pray that we have the wisdom and courage to make the right choices. I began to believe in my inner strengths, as I realized that I had the ability to survive, because my God can restore, in fact He has restored those years of abuse for me. I meditated in the things of the world day and night and worldly things are what operated in my life. I now meditate in God's Word day and night and I allow the Word to speak to my spirit, as spiritual things operate in my life. I can now inherit the things of God because I do not wrestle with my flesh and I have renewed my thinking. This relationship had me addicted to a bizarre lifestyle. This unfamiliar territory had me lost without any sense of direction. I was focused on the constant flow of illicit income, fornication, and drugs. The lust handicapped me mentally and destroyed me physically. I allowed myself to be tempted and led into a life full of distrust and dishonesty. I was quickly drawn away and enticed by worldly desires and material possessions. This lust consumed me and brought forth a life of sin and this sin when it manifested fully, was intended to kill me! Marcus had every intention to destroy me. His voice, his tone, his posture were all life threatening. The power and evil behind each blow was deadly, but I'm still here! I'm still here because of God's grace! I wish I could say that this has been an easy journey, but it was not. There were a lot of slip-ups on my part, but I learned from my mistakes. I learned through trial and error and I focused on me and the areas of my life that needed to be changed. I had to deny myself of many things, as I focused on the promises of God. And though there were nights that I cried and days that I regretted some of the decisions that I made, with help from God, I made it through some very difficult times.

Chapter 8

THE SIGNS

S-T-O-P! Stop and look both ways before crossing the street. We learned this one as a little child. This was embedded in us to protect us from getting run over. We have stop signs, which are there for us to adhere to. These signs instruct us to stop and look both ways before proceeding to cross through an intersection. And of course we have stop lights, which indicate to drivers when to stop, go, or slow down. But how often have we ran that stop sign, eagerly to get to our destination? Many of us may have even run red lights, busily talking on the cell phone or texting, not at all aware of our surroundings. The car in front of you just came to a quick stop! That other car across from you is quickly changing lanes! These are actions that have caused many accidents and several tragedies all because we were too busy to pay attention to the things going on around us and ignored the many signals that we should adhere to. We have all kind of signs posted on the road and highways to give us direction. As we travel, we see many signs that provide direction to help us get to a specific place. Of course, we all know that the speed limit signs are posted to tell us how fast to drive and other signs warn us of lane merges, road construction, and detours! But how often do we ignore the signs? We often are so busy going in our own direction, with our own agendas that we ignore the signs that are boldly placed before us to help us get to our destination. In my rush to love, I wasted too much time and I made too many mistakes. I ran the red light and went directly in to rush hour traffic. I was headed straight for destruction, simply because I ignored all the detour and caution signs that were right in front of me. I guess I was looking for some miraculous sign to forewarn me, as I ignorantly disregarded the many simple signs that were right in front of me!

You may ask or even think……. "How did it feel to be in such an abusive relationship?" It was confusing and uncomfortable! I was confused because I thought that this was love, and I was uncomfortable in this thing that I was calling love. I know that there are a lot of people who do not understand the cycle of abuse, but for those of you that do know, please also understand that this is a vicious cycle that you have the power to end.

I got caught up in all the hype and excitement. In the beginning, I was excited because I had a new man and a new attitude. I remember how we started going out on dates and we even had the late night phone calls. After months of kissing, hugging, and holding hands, the new wore off. The glitz and glamour of this love slowly faded away. I started to notice the tone of his voice getting louder and his requests turning into demands. I looked over how he planned and paid for everything. I was just enjoying the ride. Here was a man that I thought loved me and he took good care of me. He had started being just a little too physical. I remember how he would grab me when he was talking and he would make cute threats. What is cute about a threat? I never thought he was really serious, so I continued to brush it off as nothing. All my life I had waited on this love. I had yearned for this attention, and now that I had it, I was determined to hold on to it, and so I allowed the abuse to continue. At first, I thought that it was not that bad and that it would get better. This was a very uncomfortable place, but I was willing to make some adjustments, if it meant holding on to my man. I didn't know the reason behind his dysfunctional behavior, but I stayed because I cared. I did not notice how controlling he had become. Well, I did notice, but I ignored the signs. I reflect back on how he acted when we went to the club, he didn't want me to walk around a lot and he watched me everywhere I went. He started using mind games to manipulate me. He would ask a lot of questions about who I talked to and always accused me of flirting with somebody. He was jealous any time I talked to anyone other than him. This jealousy was a clear sign of insecurity and possessiveness; it had nothing to do with love. But he would always clean up his mess, with an apology and a gift. So now here I am naïve enough to be happy about an expensive gift that had no significance. The gift did make me smile, but the reality of this turmoil made me cry. This stuff, yes this stuff was so important to me, yet it was worthless and had no value. I thought this was love. It felt good and I enjoyed that feeling, even if it was just for a little while. I was so irrational and trapped up in this material gain that I was loosing the essence of myself. I remember when I use to be at the beauty shop, he would stop in and pay for my hair, bring me some lunch, and even put a few extra dollars in my pocket. I was on cloud nine, enjoying the life of a drug dealer's girlfriend. I had on a new outfit every time I stepped out. He not only paid for the outfit, but he usually picked it out! Now, that I really think about it, he always picked out my clothes, I thought it was cute then, but now I see that this was truly another form of manipulation and control. Now, I do believe that his intentions were good and he was playing the role of taking care of his girl very well, but at the end of the day I was still in an abusive relationship. I recall one particular night, I was at the club and I was in the corner dancing with my girls. My song was bumping and I was having a good time. I could see Marcus out the corner of my eye, so I kept the moves medium range. I could see him walking over my way; he came over and grabbed me by the arm, which demanded my immediate attention! I thought that this dude had lost his mind. My instant reaction was to snatch away from him and I was ready for whatever. I couldn't believe this dude had his hands on me; he had gone left on me up in the club. This was the very first time that he had come at me like this in public and I was not prepared.

He then started cussing at me, saying that he didn't want me dancing in the club like that. He accused me of flirting with some other guy. I was so confused and I tried to explain to him that it wasn't like that, but he was so mad he just left me standing there talking to myself. I knew that it was time to leave, so I walked towards the door to get in the car, but then, I saw him posted up in some other female's face.

Now, I'm thinking you're tripping on me, yet you're over here having a side conversation with some other woman. I was too hot and I was getting ready to fly off the handle, but my girl came and walked me to the door. Marcus somehow beat me to the car and was waiting on me, which I thought was strange. One way or the other he always managed to do other things and still watch my every move. I was so caught up in worrying about him being mad at me; I didn't even mention the fact of how he was talking to some other female. I saw only what I wanted to see and most of the time; denial was my best way out.

As I was getting in the car, Raymond, an old classmate leaned over in the window to see if I was okay. I guess Raymond, didn't realize how crazy Marcus was, as I nervously nodded my head and tried to brush him off. Marcus got in the car and saw Raymond talking to me. He reached under his seat and pulled a gun out on him! Yes, this dude pulled out a gun, so quickly it scared me speechless. I don't know where the gun came from, but it was right in my face pointing over at Raymond. I heard him tell this man, that he should never speak to me again and that if he didn't step back he would put a hole in him. I sat there dumbfounded. I didn't even know that he had a gun and I surely didn't think he would pull it out on somebody for such a simple gesture. I don't know which frightened me more, the fact that he had a gun or the thought of him ever pulling a gun out on me! I just prayed and wondered why I was even with a man with these types of psycho tendencies. He laid the gun down in his lap and sped off very quickly. He just start going off on me, talking about I was embarrassing him at the club. I opened my mouth to respond, but he slapped me so hard it brought tears to my eyes.

Chapter 9

DADDY'S LITTLE GIRL

"Daddy
Daddy where are you?
I am so scared and I need you to help me.
I waited for you to come and comfort me.
I needed you to tell me that everything would be alright.
In my pain, I called out for you, but you never came.
Daddy where are you?
Through my tears I cried out for you, but you never answered.
Daddy where are you?"
My heart had been broken and my feelings had been hurt.
I looked for my daddy, but I could not find him.

You see, this search for love with Marcus was my chance to be open with a man, to be loved, and to feel important. This chance for love with Marcus clouded my thoughts and I mistakenly identified the lust of my life to be the love of my life. I had so many questions.

Where was my example of love?

What is love, and what are the steps to finding true love?"

Ladies, I know that we often put so much effort into these lifeless relationships, trying to work them out like a complex math problem! I never liked math, so I skipped all the tedious and important steps trying to hurry up and get the answer. Well, with this love thing, I think I missed all the significant steps, taking leaps trying to go straight for the answers, not understanding the importance of taking things one step at a time. I wasn't sure about the process of a real relationship or the perception of love. I thought I had the answers, but I didn't know how to apply the concepts and now that I was being tested, I couldn't even pass the test! I was failing this course with flying colors!

I remember how desperately I wanted my daddy to love and protect me, as most little girls do. I just wanted to be loved and I wanted to give love. There was emptiness in my heart. I had a void that I tried to fill with love under false pretenses. I'm sure that there are a lot of women who are not aware of the voids and discrepancies that leave them vulnerable to this love under false pretenses. I was open to this artificial love, because of the lack of security and love that I so desperately wanted from my daddy. This unhealthy concept of fatherhood followed me for many years. I now know that there is a Father that cares for me and will always love me. He is a Father to the fatherless. He is my God and He will supply all my needs. As I began to look for Him with all my heart and all my soul I found a love like no other. I found that love and that protection of my daddy. I loved him and he loved me back! The emptiness in my heart was overflowing with peace, love, and joy. I am no longer bound in sadness and unhealthy relationships, but I now have an intimate relationship with the Father. All this time I was looking for a love that was right in front of me, but I was so caught up in worldly activities to see the true essence of this love!

I was in a false love, looking for truth. I was trying to make this wrong thing right and this bad outcome turn out as good. I was tempted by the desires of my flesh and trapped in my sin. I somehow stayed in this relationship so long that I began to make excuses for Marcus's behavior. I carried the resentment in my heart for my father for so many years and I blamed him for not loving me. My pain had been exposed and identified as a target of weakness and vulnerability. I was surely under attack and I didn't have enough wisdom to identify the works of the devil or the tools that I needed to fight him back. I thought I needed the love from this man and I mistakenly identified his touch and temperance for love everlasting. To the hungry, even what is bitter taste sweet (Proverbs 27:7). The Bible tells us that Jesus came that we might have and enjoy life. He provides a way of escape, though living in my sin; I wasn't looking for a way of escape. I was just looking for a way to live comfortably while I was in sin. I was looking for a way to validate this false sense of security. This false sense of security had me scared and confused. I was lonely, but I wasn't alone. God carried me, even in my mess. He carried me through some very difficult times. I had a thirst for love and an appetite for success, but this experimentation of love with Marcus did not quench my thirst or help my hunger. I finally realized that I was feasting at the wrong table and anxiously partaking from the wrong bread.

I grew up in a two-parent home, with my mother and stepfather. It was the ideal setup. I was the oldest of four children. I was the only one of my siblings that had a different dad. My mother was married to my step dad and he was a great provider. He took very good care of us. He actually was the only dad I really knew. He made sure we had plenty of food and all the bills were paid. Yet, as a child there was still something missing. I still wanted to be hugged. I still wanted to be encouraged and loved. I could always feel the difference between me and my other three siblings. He didn't intentionally treat us any different, but I always recognized the difference. To an adult, this may seem minor, but to a child this is a major thing. I had to deal with a lot of misunderstood emotions as I longed for a relationship with my biological father. Mr. Jerry Smith was my biological father and everyone knew me as Mr. Smith's child. It was complex for me because; I carried the label of Mr. Smith's daughter. I was always uncomfortable and signaled out. My daddy was alive and well. He was in the same town as I was, but he never did anything for me. He was well known in our neighborhood and it seemed like he had time for everybody but me.

He was a chronic drug user and an alcoholic, but I loved him, because he was my daddy. Every time I asked him for something he would tell me to come back later and of course when I would come back, he was not there when I returned. I remember how I would spend the night at my grandma's house just to be close to him, but he would never be at home. He would have his girlfriends to take me to the store or I would just hang out with my grandma all day. I was actually okay with this, because I was just happy to be over to my daddy's house. He would often come in and out of the house with his girlfriends, but never paid any attention to me. He never asked me how I was doing or how I felt. I don't think we ever had a real conversation. He didn't even come to my high school graduation or my college graduation. I hand delivered him a graduation invitation, with no real expectation that he would actually attend, just a glimpse of hope that he would at least consider it. I wanted him to be proud me. I needed him to love me and I prayed for him to comfort me. I just wanted some attention and love from my dad, but that was something that I never got. He never told me that he loved me. He never hugged me or even acknowledged any of my accomplishments. My dad paid more attention to the drugs and the streets then he did to me, and I hopelessly longed for his approval and his love. I waited for his love that I never got to know. This kind of love I had never experienced. That love, that genuine love that every daddy's little girl needs. That everlasting, unconditional love from my daddy, that long lasting, unexplainable love. I never got that love! I yearned for this kind of love, all my life. I wanted my daddy's love, I wanted his touch, and I needed his approval. I thought I had found this love in Marcus. I went straight for that love and that secure covering that I thought I had missed, but I was driving full speed with my hands in the air and my foot on the gas, not realizing that I was in the wrong lane!

As a little girl, I experienced a lot of hurtful words..........

Sticks and stones may break my bones, but words will never hurt me.

This was not true for me. As a little girl trying to fit in, words do hurt! I know as parents we try to give our children little encouraging bullets to help them survive, but as a child, words do hurt. I wanted acceptance from my friends, yet I was experiencing a lot of rejection. My identity was tampered and my self esteem was damaged. I was always the butt of the joke because I am so dark skinned. At that time, black was not so beautiful and being from the projects didn't help much.

Marcus made me feel pretty. He paid so much attention to me. At this time in my life, I thought that was important. He offered me a bogus brand of what I thought was real love. You know that love that looks just like the real thing and from a distance you can't tell if it is the real thing or just a knock off. But usually if you look at it, really examine it; you can tell that it's a fake. The stitches are different, the texture is different, but most of all the quality is different. I knew that the quality of love that Marcus offered was flawed, but I wanted it so bad I carried it around perpetrating it as an original. I really couldn't distinguish genuine love from fake love because for me it all looked the same. In my eyes, it appeared to be the real thing. The love that he gave looked just like that love that I longed for as a little girl. It felt so good and safe. I was awkwardly comfortable in this kind of love. I was secure in this love, and all the time I was lost in this love because I never knew love. I thought Marcus loved me. He always told me that he was so proud of me. He hugged me and he told me that he loved me. He provided a false sense of security, which impaired my judgment even the more. It seemed like he had altered his schedule and adjusted his life just right for me to fit in. This man gave me his undivided attention and he always had time just for me. He always complimented me in front of his family and his friends. This always made me feel so appreciated and loved. He told me that I was beautiful and that he loved me. I didn't have this type of attention from any man growing up. I didn't know what it was like to be loved and appreciated by a man. And when I got it, it felt so good. I felt good about myself and proud to have this man recognize me. I thought he wanted to change and he told me that he would, but he never did. He had a lot of issues to resolve, which were there before I even came into the picture. I just became a part of his unresolved issues. I began to label his control as compassion and his lies for love. I loved too hard and I was scared to give up on a love that had already given up on me. I was so emotionally damaged and I didn't want to miss this opportunity for love and affection. I made myself believe that this relationship would work. I continued to press on trying to make this last! I continuously tried to prove to myself that the direction of this relationship would eventually turn itself around. I wanted even more to prove to him that I was a good girlfriend and that I was worth loving. I know that this sounds some what outlandish, but at that point in my life I lived off environmental stressors and emotional highs. I tried to keep busy during the day, in order to forget the stress and misery that waited for me at home. I smiled all day at school, but as soon as class ended, my smile was turned upside down. The feeling of the unknown was too overwhelming as I tried to figure out his mood for the day. My place for peace and relaxation was instantly turned into a place of fear and frustration. To my surprise, I would turn the knob and there he sat, with a smile. Today would be a good day!

I had no spiritual foundation and no Godly revelation, but me and Marcus had a good relationship. *I thought!* But as good as I thought it was my good thing came to an end! I truly believe that the relationship I had, well the relationship that I didn't have with my dad affected my decision making with men and how I viewed life and loving. I try not to make excuses for my past decisions, nor am I expecting sympathy for my past mistakes. This is just part of my personal justification for a life lived in sin and defeat, with no sense of direction.

I couldn't figure out which direction to go. I often found myself going in circles, just wanting to be happy! I got in this relationship thinking I had found happiness and satisfaction. I expected for him to make me happy. I constantly worked on this relationship trying to make it work for me. I knew in the beginning that this man was no good for me, but I was just hoping that he would change and besides I was just happy to have a man! Maybe he would change?

Is change possible?
If anyone is in Christ, he is a new creation, the old has gone, and the new has come. (II Corinthian 5:17)

What about happiness? Is happiness available?
I know that there is nothing better for man than to be happy and do good while they live (Ecc 3:12).

What is happy?
Webster's dictionary defines happy as a feeling of pleasure. It is when we are satisfied with all the right things in our life

I just wanted to be H-A-P-P-Y! I wanted to be happy in my relationships and I connected happiness to a man. Many times we are forming relationships hoping that the other person will make us happy. Of course women we do not want to just exist, we want to be happy in any relationship! I deserve to be happy! You deserve to be happy. I feel that if I give happiness and love I want to get some happiness and love back! Happiness is a good thing; in fact it is a very good thing and is an aspect that should be a part of any relationship. The joy of the Lord is my strength. He says that He has left peace and happiness, here with us. Happiness is made up of peace, smiles, and joy. But we must be a happy person before entering into any relationship. It is an emotion from within and no man should be held responsible for the happiness of another. We do want him to contribute to making us happy, but is it fair to put this great responsibility on a man? I learned a long time ago that my trust and supply are in God, not man. I understand that any relationship takes time, patience, and love. Through much prayer and consecration, God made all the changes that needed to be made, as I learned to build on the concepts of patience and love. I accepted this relationship as a learning process as I pressed forward. I pressed forward with help from my family and friends. My mother was my greatest supporter and she always encouraged me. Her prayers sustained me through the years, as she planted the seed of happiness, love, and wisdom. Her love continued during my troubled relationship, as she constantly watered and nurtured my insecurities, assuring me that God would provide me with increase and happiness. I remember discussing with my mom the hopes of one day finding a good man, a *Husband!* So many of us sit back and daydream about our perfect man! I know I'm not the only one that has described that husband in detail, during those intimate conversations with our girlfriends. I too, longed for that knight in shining armor! Even as a little girl, I had that fairytale expectation of that perfect man. There is only one PERFECT man! Every good and perfect gift is from above (James 1:17). I was on a scavenger hunt looking for love and expecting happiness. I was disappointed with the love that I found and not satisfied with the happiness I had made. Ladies, as we slow down long enough to unwrap the gifts that God has given each of us, we will receive direction. As He orders our steps, we will step out into a love and happiness ordained by God. Do you understand the value of preparation time? It is so vital that we take advantage of the preparation time, which is intended to prepare us for our next season, for our next relationship. For some reason, it seemed to me that some people's lives just happened to turn out good for them. But for me, I tried to make good things happen in my life. It took me a long time to understand the unspeakable joy of "Letting go and letting God!" I had to stop trying so hard to make things happen, because even when I thought I had all the ingredients to make something happen, once pressure was applied to my situation, I folded. I now just sit back, read the Word, pray the Word, and speak the Word over my life. I have learned to allow Him to do what He does best…BE GOD!!!

But before I learned to let go and let God, I did make some mistakes and I had a lot of issues. At a very young age I made an investment. I invested my hope, efforts, and time into Marcus. This investment did not produce any profits for me. What profits a man to gain the world, yet loose his soul? (Matthew 16:26) Each negative word and physical confrontation was a withdrawal, which caused a decrease in my passion and my desire for life. I now know that I must invest in the kingdom of God. I have experienced true love, the love of Christ, that agape love, which is an unconditional and totally selfless love. I can now understand how I misinterpreted love. I misunderstood man's love for a woman. The error of my ways was a direct result of sexual sin and lust. I continued to play with sin and a spirit of death was knocking at my door. I pulled away from the voice of God many times, trying to satisfy my flesh. It was a foolish thing to ignore the voice of God as I continued to feed myself band-aid messages. These messages were just enough to cover up the scar and soothe the pain.

"God knows my heart."

"God if you get me out of this one, I will……

"God will forgive me"

"I do go to church, but….

As wicked things and dishonest situations continued to show up in my life, I was bewildered as to what I was doing so wrong. I was trying to have an unlawful relationship with this man, but all along I was neglecting God and not obeying any of His commandments. I was trying to fix the situation, but I never repented for my sins. I had sentenced myself to my own private hell and I was wallowing in self-pity and regret. These self-inflicted wounds caused me a lot of pain, as I continued to look for this lost love! In my quest to find love, I found this intimate message and I want to share it with each of you. I implore you to study this intimate message. Find each scripture and see how this Word will minister to your hearts and heal your pain. Listen to His voice as He says "I love you!" I have finally found that love I had been looking for and longing for all my life. This love it hugged me, it comforted me, and it protected me! Enjoy His message to you and read slowly, take pleasure in the true essence of love and fellowship with the Father!

Kamekio Danielle

An Intimate Message from God to You
Father's Love Letter

My Child
You may not know me,
but I know everything about you.
Psalm 139:1

I know when you sit down and when you rise up.
Psalm 139:2

I am familiar with all your ways.
Psalm 139:3

Even the very hairs on your head are numbered.
Matthew 10:29-31

For you were made in my image.
Genesis 1:27

In me you live and move and have your being.
Acts 17:28

For you are my offspring.
Acts 17:28

I knew you even before you were conceived.
Jeremiah 1:4-5

I chose you when I planned creation.
Ephesians 1:11-12

You were not a mistake,
for all your days are written in my book.
Psalm 139:15-16

I determined the exact time of your birth
and where you would live.
Acts 17:26

You are fearfully and wonderfully made.
Psalm 139:14

I knit you together in your mother's womb.
Psalm 139:13

And brought you forth on the day you were born.
Psalm 71:6

I have been misrepresented
by those who don't know me.
John 8:41-44

I am not distant and angry,
but am the complete expression of love.
1 John 4:16

And it is my desire to lavish my love on you.
1 John 3:1

Simply because you are my child
and I am your Father.
1 John 3:1

I offer you more than your earthly father ever could.
Matthew 7:11

Kamekio Danielle

For I am the perfect father.
Matthew 5:48

Every good gift that you receive comes from my hand.
James 1:17

For I am your provider and I meet all your needs.
Matthew 6:31-33

My plan for your future has always been filled with hope.
Jeremiah 29:11

Because I love you with an everlasting love.
Jeremiah 31:3

My thoughts toward you are countless
as the sand on the seashore.
Psalms 139:17-18

And I rejoice over you with singing.
Zephaniah 3:17

I will never stop doing good to you.
Jeremiah 32:40

For you are my treasured possession.
Exodus 19:5

I desire to establish you
with all my heart and all my soul.
Jeremiah 32:41

And I want to show you great and marvelous things.
Jeremiah 33:3

If you seek me with all your heart,
you will find me.
Deuteronomy 4:29

Delight in me and I will give you
the desires of your heart.
Psalm 37:4

For it is I who gave you those desires.
Philippians 2:13

I am able to do more for you
than you could possibly imagine.
Ephesians 3:20

For I am your greatest encourager.
2 Thessalonians 2:16-17

I am also the Father who comforts you
in all your troubles.
2 Corinthians 1:3-4

When you are brokenhearted,
I am close to you.
Psalm 34:18

As a shepherd carries a lamb,
I have carried you close to my heart.
Isaiah 40:11

One day I will wipe away
every tear from your eyes.
Revelation 21:3-4

Kamekio Danielle

And I'll take away all the pain
you have suffered on this earth.
Revelation 21:3-4

I am your Father, and I love you
even as I love my son, Jesus.
John 17:23

For in Jesus, my love for you is revealed.
John 17:26

He is the exact representation of my being.
Hebrews 1:3

He came to demonstrate that I am for you,
not against you.
Romans 8:31

And to tell you that I am not counting your sins.
2 Corinthians 5:18-19

Jesus died so that you and I could be reconciled.
2 Corinthians 5:18-19

His death was the ultimate expression
of my love for you.
1 John 4:10

I gave up everything I loved
that I might gain your love.
Romans 8:31-32

If you receive the gift of my son Jesus,
you receive me.
1 John 2:23

And nothing will ever separate you
from my love again.
Romans 8:38-39

Come home and I'll throw the biggest party
heaven has ever seen.
Luke 15:7

I have always been Father,
and will always be Father.
Ephesians 3:14-15

My question is…
Will you be my child?
John 1:12-13

I am waiting for you.
Luke 15:11-32

Love, Your Dad
Almighty God

© Father Heart Communications (Barry Adams)

Chapter 10

LOOKING FOR LOVE

Abuse, whether physical or mental can consume you if you let it. It can consume your thoughts, your actions, and your responses. Abuse affects your entire lifestyle! I still blame myself for looking for love in all the wrong places. I did not know love nor did I understand how to love. I labeled his control as concern. The way he treated me sometimes, often led me to believe that he was concerned about me and my happiness. I began to accept his excuses and I excused his baffling behaviors. I continued blindly in a relationship, knowing that I need to leave, yet I still ignorantly believed that he was deserving of my love. Even with all the bad things that happened, I put forth extra efforts because I thought I loved this man and I didn't understand why he just couldn't love me back! I remembered how it started, but I wasn't sure how it would end. For that matter, I wasn't sure how I would end up, or which direction my life was headed. Somehow, I made the choice to choose this person to be in my life. I never expected for him to be abusive, but because I chose to stay with him, there were consequences that I endured. I must say that the results of my decision ended in consequences that I was not prepared for. And though I was young, with little knowledge about abusive relationships and controlling boyfriends, I was still old enough to know better and intelligent enough to do better. I was so busy trying to develop a relationship with this man, that I really didn't have time to develop myself. I should have been trying to develop my values, my beliefs, and my standards. I suffered physical and mental abuse for a long time. Some people are knowledgeable about the affects of physical and mental abuse. They are able to identify the victims because of the black eyes and broken bones, but domestic abuse comes in all forms of control and hurt. The physical abuse I endured was a very painful experience and often times left visible marks. The emotional abuse did not leave any visible marks, but there were internal scars, which have taken longer to heal. I knew that this abuse was not normal, and it was not healthy, yet I chose to stay in an unhealthy relationship! These unhealthy patterns of behaviors were used as power plays to manipulate and control me and I was foolish enough to call it love. If you or someone you know is experiencing any type of abuse, I urge you to seek help!

I have seen many people in all walks of life become detrimentally affected by this dirty little secret, called abuse. Abuse does not differentiate between black and white, rich or poor. It doesn't just happen to tall or short women or fat or skinny women. Abuse is a one size fits all monster and can only be defeated, when an individual is equipped with the proper tools and weapons to fight back! As revelation and courage comes, you empower yourself to confront this situation and move forward with your life. But my question is "why do so many women feel that they must keep this a secret?" "Are we condoning this abuse by keeping silent?" We keep this intimate detail of our relationship to ourselves for so long, until it destroys us, and many times it also destroys our families. There are women out there who are being abused! Nevertheless they are trying to maintain this oath of secrecy in hopes to save their marriage or their relationships, but fail to realize that all the while they are loosing themselves. Abuse should never be a secret! It is time for women to expose it for what it is! We must deal with this situation before it deals with us. A lot of women sit in the abuse trying to figure out what to do next. They feel alone, misunderstood, and neglected. These emotions are mixed with fear, hope, and love. We fear what will happen if we leave, and all the time we continue to hope that it will get better if we stay, because we love him and we want our relationships to work. Sometimes we hold on to this secret for so long that we don't recognize how our lives are dramatically affected. Many times our lives are lost, all because we sat in our misery one day too long. This secret, whispers to us during the day and screams at us in the night. Don't hesitate to let the secret out and realize that abuse is very real. If you too are going through know that you are not alone. It is time to stop tip toeing around this issue and call it exactly what it is. It is abuse! We must learn how to talk about abuse and seek some professional help. Many victims have tried for many years to bury it and many have tried to forget it, but have never forgiven. It is time to forgive your abuser and move on with your lives. The word tells us to be kind and compassionate to one another, forgiving each other, just as in Christ God forgave you (Ephesians 4:32). The abused woman just might be you. It could be your mother, your sister, or your friend, so we have to lift each other up in prayer and not allow past hurts to overpower us or alter our entire lifestyle.

Although, the hitting stopped, the pain followed me for many years. This experience was very damaging and it could have destroyed me, if I had let it. I thought I had gotten past the abusive relationship that I was in years ago. I really tried to push pass the memories of my past. I tried to love again, but the wounds were still open and the pain was still there. I know now that I never really healed. I just tried to deal with it, but it actually had started to deal with me. As I tried to move on with my life, I began to add the weight of the world to the load I was already carrying. The load got heavier as the years passed. Time did not heal my pain and each reminder I would see in a movie or in a news report about a woman in an abusive relationship, was like picking at an open wound and I would cringe. All these years I had ignored the damage that this abuse had caused. I neglected to face the reality of my pass and the memories had begun to resurface. It spread through my mind like an infection and I didn't know how to treat it.

I had suppressed these issues for so long and I was now afraid to admit that I had suffered this type of ill treatment. How do you bring up old hurts and try to talk to people about it? How do you tell someone that I was abused years ago, but it feels like it was yesterday? I couldn't sleep and when I did go to bed, I had nightmares. These are the things that I decided to bury and not talk to anyone about. I thought it would be ridiculous and shameful so I tried to continue with my life as usual. As I watched the news, I continued to see women who were being killed by their lovers, boyfriends, or even their husbands. Each report was very, very upsetting for me. I could feel a piece of my pain in each story. I never really thought of myself as a victim of domestic violence. I was too established to be caught up in anything like that, but the truth is, yes I was once a victim! I know now that I am a survivor! I survived through all of the life threatening behaviors and attacks on my life. If you are living in a domestic violence situation, I want you to know that there is professional help available and there is a way of escape, but you have to first want help. It is vital that we seek advice from a well informed family member or from a professional. We often struggle to try and understand how to reach out for help, as we ask ourselves why are we staying in these abusive situations. I believe that fear is the number one reason that women are staying in these abusive relationships.

The fear of what you might ask….The fears of being alone. No one wants to be alone or think of a life with no companionship. Being alone often makes you feel worthless and incapable of a loving relationship. Being alone makes you think of growing old by yourself, and you begin to question your ability to have that happily ever after.

The fear of leaving love and not being able to find love again or being able to give love again. Some women often feel damaged and reluctant to commit to a real, open, and loving relationship. The fear of loosing our stuff! In many relationships, we have accumulated so many things together; we don't want to just leave it. The stuff, that bedroom suite, living room furniture, or dinette set that we hold so dear to our hearts can be replaced, you can't! We sit and rationalize why we should stay, knowing that it's past time for us to go and not look back.

I was too embarrassed to actually ask for help. I wanted this relationship and I continued to run back to it, although it was a lost cause. I tried to hide the hopelessness and I failed to get the help that I needed. Ultimately I made a lot of bad decisions and I went through a lot of trials, before I realized that I had the power to end this cycle of abuse. I constantly tried to fix it, to make it work and no matter how hard I tried, this relationship just would not work out for me. I wanted his love so much that I let his ongoing lies get me through some very sad days, but deep in my spirit the truth was staring me in my face. Like myself, there are other women out there who are living in shame and embarrassment, accepting the lies while ignoring the truths that are staring them right in the face. Some women are feeling guilty because they have allowed this abuse to continue in their lives for too long. One year too long, one week too long, one day too long, one hour too long, or one minute too long! I too buried the hurt and smiled through the pain, for longer than I should have. I lived in humiliation and distress for a very long time. I am at fault because I knew that it was wrong, but I didn't understand the seriousness of my situation. I looked over the wrong because I wanted so bad to make it right. I recognized that it was abuse, yet I allowed it to continue in my life. During my relationship with Marcus, I was in college and too scared to tell anyone. I was too afraid of what people would think and what they would say about a 23 year old woman in this kind of situation. I never reached out to anyone. Yes, we do have young women, teenagers and college girls that are in abusive relationships. They are staying in this abuse, making excuses, and calling it love. The operative question is, "how do we fight this cycle of abuse?" We have to come together and empower our youth and our women about the signs of abuse. We need to profile an abusive man before he becomes our man. It is important to spend time with him and find out what his interests are. During those long phone conversations, listen to his life goals and take a mental note of his actions. Take time to understand his perspective on life and his gestures during your playful encounters and your heated moments.

I never really dealt with the internal scars that were left behind. I just thought I could get over it. I somehow thought that I could forget this part of my life. I ran from the memories of my past for many years. I convinced myself that this was all water under the bridge. It was just one of the many mistakes that I had made. I never made any efforts to understand it or confront it; I just subconsciously lived in fear and denial. I wanted to close this chapter of my life, but each news story or *Lifetime* movie would give life to this past pain. Each time I would hear about some young girl or some woman living life so wrecklessly, would remind me of the wreckless life that I once lived and how blessed I am to have survived. I was even more disturbed, because I began to see family members and friends accept this abuse as normal. They would tell me every detail of their stories, lost in a love full of fear and deceit. It was always so much drama and I could vividly see the horror of the story play by play as they would tell me how their husband, boyfriend, or lover had slapped, punched and choked them. I would listen as they talked about their experience with simplicity, not realizing the seriousness of these offenses. The sad part was that they would justify and accept this abuse all in the name of love. I look back now I know that it was God's grace that kept me, but where sin increased, grace increased all the more (Romans 5:20). I too, once justified and accepted abuse as part of my relationship. In my past relationship there was a lot of pain and misunderstood emotions. The pain that I thought I left in my past began to build up and spill over into my current life. This eruption of past pain and misunderstood emotions caused additional damage to the pain that I thought was gone. This pain and this shame, multiplied and it began to surface.

Through the years I attempted several relationships, but I failed at quite a few. I was not interested in any type of commitment that required emotional attachment. I preferred a reserved association, as I maintained friendships with no strings attached, no commitments, and definitely no love. I had been hurt in such an unimaginable way that I never wanted to trust a man again. I thought I would never say those three words again "I Love You." These words were taboo in my mind and I kept my feelings guarded, as I loved from a distance.

Imagine a man that comes into your life that is willing to hold you, after your unexplainable nightmares. A man, who really cares for you, comforts you, inspires you and consoles you through the hardest times in your life. I met a man that truly transformed my life and my pursuit for love began. I was able to disarm my feelings, trust again and love again. I moved cautiously into this new relationship, but this new love helped me to break down the emotional walls that I had built. My new love, my husband, he helped me to surpass my boundaries and overcome my fears. He embraced my pain and he untangled my mixed emotions and this helped me to love him like he deserved to be loved. I somehow, was still holding on to past hurts and I can remember times when my husband would do or say certain things, and I would become very irritated and defensive. I automatically started to guard my feelings and defend my heart, because I was afraid of what would happen next. The agony and the pain started up again, and though I tried to cover it up, it was uncovered and began to affect my every day life.

When me and my husband did have any type of disagreement, or if I just thought he did or didn't do something, I wanted to fight. I wanted to fight him, because I still had this built up defense were I just knew that this is where the arguments would lead to. I reflected on my past relationship and remembered that the argument would only last so long, before the fight began! I knew that it was not okay to fight, but somehow my mind triggered to defense mode and I prepared myself for the worse! I knew that it was wrong, but I still expected it. I didn't even realize that I had become this person. My husband is tough, but tender. I remember the look in his eyes when I first drew back to hit him. It was a very surprised look! He had a look of disappointment on his face, as he grabbed my arm to stop me from hitting him. I was mentally stuck in the mindset of abuse. He made it very clear to me that day that we would not fight and that he would never stoop to hitting me. I knew that my husband would never hit me, but the pain from my past was coming forth. It was happening so fast that I didn't realize what I was doing! I was tearing down my house with my own hands! This past hurt was trying to dominate my life and destroy my marriage. I knew that I had to take authority over this situation once and for all. I began to seek out help in my local church and talk to my husband about these pint up feelings. I had never told him about my abusive past, but when I did he consoled me and comforted me through my recovery. Since then I have learned how to love and how to redirect my anger. I thank God that I now know what love is and how love truly feels. I have also learned other ways to deal with my frustrations. I do not hit my husband and he has never hit me. I only did what I knew to do at that time, which was to defend myself, and react physically. I had to admit to myself that I had allowed this abuse to consume me for many years. I had to recognize how this past experience was affecting my current lifestyle, and I had to accept some professional help and expert advice, as I took steps towards my freedom.

I had been angry at myself for a very long time and I was angry at Marcus for even longer. I was angry because I was hurt. I was angry at me, because I allowed this hurt in my life and I allowed this man to mistreat and abuse me. I continued with the excuses, because I wanted to be loved and I latched on to what I thought love was. But one day, I decided that I would not allow this experience to overshadow me any longer. I got a revelation and I realized that I had the authority to speak to my situation. My bible tells me that "IF" I can believe, "ALL" things are possible. I had to learn to believe and allow God to take care of the when, who, where and how? I have learned that the world will grade you, but God will grace you.

Chapter 11

STARTING OVER

To every thing there is a season, and a time to every purpose under the heaven. – (Ecclesiastes 3:1)

I applied to Thurgood Marshall Law School my junior year in college. I had taken the law school admission test (LSAT) and passed with flying colors. I was excitedly waiting on my acceptance letter. I was almost at the end of my senior year in college and the day finally came. I got the letter in the mail! It was addressed to me, from Thurgood Marshall School of Law! I had this letter in my hand and was so nervous to open it up, but I was anxious to see the results. I opened it up and to my surprise I had been accepted! I wanted all my life to be a lawyer. I wanted to be the change that everyone needed to see. I wanted to excel high above the expectations of the girl from the hood. This was my childhood dream and I always told everyone in my neighborhood that I was going to go to law school. I worked eagerly through four years of college, preparing my self for the next level of my education. I was studying hard at night and juggling a man during the day. I was determined to be a lawyer. I knew that being a lawyer would equip me to be able to take care of my mom and my siblings, as every youngster vows to do as a child. I knew that I would make so much money, and I could buy my mamma that house that she always talked about. I always wanted to take care of her and provide for her, like she did for me all those years. I guess I didn't realize I had to take care of me first. I was on my way up, but my lifestyle was pointing in a downward direction. Yet, I was still so excited about going to law school. I shared this good news with Marcus and like a leach; he leached on and encouraged me to move forward. He was ready to pack up his stuff. He was all for me going to law school, so that I could defend his criminal acts. He always said that I would be his ticket out and I think this made me press even harder. I just wanted to save him. I wanted to help him. I wanted to change him, but only God has the power to change a man's heart. I did finally realize that he wasn't trying to change or help himself. I was dreaming of a better life for him. I was planning for him, but he had to plan and dream for himself. He said that he would get a job and that we would marry and have kids. I was so overjoyed about law school and telling my mom about the news that I ignorantly started to agree with this bizarre life he was laying out for me. I was moving around fervently, preparing for graduation and trying to move forward, but something was not right about this transition. Lately, I could not sleep. I could not eat and I needed some time to myself. I took a long drive and I ended up at the mall. I don't know why I was going to the mall; I didn't have any money and I had no intentions of buying anything. I was just in the mall. I had been there for about two hours and I was just walking and thinking. I sat down and I watched as people shopped. I watched and I saw people who were pleased and playing and enjoying each other. There were so many couples holding hands, smiling, and laughing as they went about their merry ways. It was at that moment, that I realized that the cupid phase of my relationship had come to an end! I felt like I was living in the wrong life and I was determined to find a better way of living, a better love, a better me. I had to get back on the track that my mom had worked so hard to put me on. I had to stay focused on my goals and my aspirations. I had gotten lost in a world with limited opportunities and I was full of excuses and lies. I was tired of the excuses and sick of the lies. I was finally ready to detach myself from this very disturbing relationship and live life on my on terms! I had to make some new plans and find my purpose. I knew that God had a plan for my life, but how could He fulfill His plan for my life, if I was not abiding by the rules of the Word and not in position to receive. I was tired of feeling my way around in the dark, taking small steps and hoping not to stumble. I was tired of making up the rules as I went along and praying that God would sprinkle a few graces over my sin. I was sleeping with this man, loving this man, but all the while denying The Man! I had given away my valuable and precious jewels anticipating love and respect in return. This man didn't love me nor did he respect me! I knew that this man was no good for me, but because of the physical attraction and the sexual distraction I had lost focus. I began to focus on what was important and I refused to continue to go back and make up, just to break up all over again. I was tired of constantly going around in circles, back and forth again in a life of sin with the same man and the same problems. *If you want a different result, you must do something different (Einstein).*

Precious Promises:

In my heart I felt the sentence of death. But this happened that I might not rely on myself but on God, who raises the dead. He has delivered me from such a deadly peril, and he will deliver us. On him I have set my hope that he will continue to deliver me (2 Corinthian 1:9-10).

For wisdom will enter my heart, and knowledge will be pleasant to my soul. Discretion will protect me, and understanding will guard me. Wisdom will save me from the ways of wicked men, from men whose words are perverse (Proverbs 2:10-11)

I was suddenly in survival mode, as I passed by an army recruiting station. I stood there for a moment and then decided to go in. I heard a man ask me if he could help me. His voice seemed to echo in the back of my mind and again he asked if he could help me. "Why am I standing in this office?" I asked myself this question and I turned to leave, but my feet would not move. I opened my mouth to say no, but instead I said I want to enlist in the army! I could not believe the words that were coming out of my mouth. I was saying that I wanted to join the United States Army! The military is considered to be a place for rigorous activity and disciplined people. You are expected to sacrifice yourself, defend your battle buddy, and fight for your country. Most people thought that I would be afraid to go and that I would never survive the tough cycles of boot camp. I had been in a boot camp for the last year, filled with rigorous activities and survival techniques. I had tried to leave this relationship from all angles, so this was my last option. The military was my permission slip to get out of this abusive lifestyle. This was my chance to start over and get some things back on track. This opportunity presented itself to me and it was a very attractive proposition at this time in my life. As I stood there, I knew that I was making a decision to leave home. I was afraid, but there was this indescribable peace, and I knew that everything would be alright. I was a little scared because I would have to leave my friends and my family. My thoughts were racing and my mind was trying to figure it out, but my heart knew that this was something that I had to do. If I didn't go, how would I end up? What direction was my life going? What was the quality of life that I had been living? I thought about the stuff I had to give up and the things I had to leave behind, but these things had no value. I had to realize that my life was the most valuable thing I had. I was not taking care of me. I didn't even understand me anymore. I don't even know if I loved me anymore. It took about an hour to complete my paperwork. I felt so comfortable signing my name on the dotted line; this was my first real sign of progress. I felt like I was getting ready to step in to a whole new world. I was giving up my opportunity to go to law school, but I was giving myself a chance to have and enjoy my life. The recruiter asked me when I wanted to leave. I didn't even have to give this much thought. I knew that graduation was next week and I didn't have much time. I would graduate on a Saturday and I wanted to leave out on that Sunday! There was no time to consult with anyone or think about the decision. It was past time for me to go as far away as I could. I nervously, shared this news with my mother and my family. I could hear the sadness in her voice because I decided to leave, but I saw the joy in her eyes because I had to leave! We both knew that I had to get away from this environment and purge myself of this ludicrous thing I was calling love. Leaving my hometown and packing up my life and going off to an unknown place, was a very hard thing for me to do. I remember packing my bags, as I prepared for this journey by myself. There would be no friends, no family, and I would have no one to talk to. I was zipping up my bag and I reached over to my dresser and grabbed my Bible. And as I placed my Bible in my bag, I knew that He would be my friend, my family, and my help! "Surely I am with you always, to the very end of the age (Matthew 28:20)."

What was my next move?

I received orders to mobilize. This mobilization was a tactile move, which included a 25 mile road march. And though I despised road marches my entire military career, I knew that there was something great connected to this move. This journey was designed to move me from where I was to where God needed me to be. My military experience taught me that I had to always be aware of my surroundings and always be preapared for the next move. Before we were able to make any moves; we received specific instructions on the details of the mission and instructions on how to navigate through the terrain. After receiving detailed instructions of the mission, I had to execute and move forward. I had to pack up my ruck sack with everything that I would possibly need for this 25 mile road march. I had my water, toiletries, snacks, extra socks, and some food! Any and everything that I needed had to be packed tight in that ruck sack on my back. I remember before each mission, we received our final instructions; we then tightened up our boots, and got to moving.

On this journey, my journey to healing, every step that I took was a step of faith, as I was so sure in my heart that the love I hoped for, for so many years would soon manifest. God said for me to tighten up my boot straps and everything that I needed was on my back in my ruck sack…my B-I-B-L-E! And though I despised the journey, I still had to go. I am now on the other side of the trials and the tribulations. I am enjoying the love that I hoped for and looked for, for so many years. I have fallen in love with Jesus and I let no one or nothing separate me from that everlasting, unconditional love. I took this journey, but I had to move slow, taking it all one step at a time, following the instructions given! What is your next move?

Be sure to look directly at your situation and speak with authority, just as Jesus did! "Get behind me, Satan!" You are a stumbling block to me; you do not have in mind the things of God, but the things of men (Matthew 16:23)." So, I spoke to my situation, this thing that was weighing me down and holding me back, and I told it to get behind me. I commanded that it get out of my way. I have followed the instructions that were given; therefore I am always three steps ahead of the enemy! The enemy is now behind me, so he doesn't know what my next move will be; all he knows is that I am moving. I encourage each of you to keep it moving!

Of course, I didn't know it then, but now I know that joining the military was all in God's plan for my life. "I will instruct you and teach you in the way you should go" (Psalm 32:8). This decision to join the United States Army changed my life forever.

Precious Promises:

For if you forgive men when they sin against you, your heavenly Father will also forgive you. But if you do not forgive men their sins, your Father will not forgive your sins (Matthew 6:14-15)

Create in me a pure heart, O God, and renew a steadfast spirit within me. Do not cast me from your presence or take your Holy Spirit from me. Restore to me the joy of your salvation and grant me a willing spirit, to sustain me. (Psalm 51:10-12)

Then I acknowledged my sin to you and did not cover up my iniquity. I said, "I will confess my transgressions to the LORD "— and you forgave the guilt of my sin. (Psalm 32:5)

Do not judge and you will not be judged? Do not condemn, and you will not be condemned. Forgive, and you will be forgiven. (Luke 6:37)

"But if a wicked man turns away from all the sins he has committed and keeps all my decrees and does what is just and right, he will surely live; he will not die. None of the offenses he has committed will be remembered against him. Because of the righteous things he has done, he will live. (Ezekiel 18:21)

Chapter 12

FORGIVENESS

And when you stand praying, if you hold anything against anyone, forgive him, so that your Father in Heaven may forgive your sin
(Mark 11:25).

Though I have not forgotten what Marcus did to me, I have forgiven the sin behind the man. It took me a long time, but I had to stop being angry at him. I had to learn how to not resent him. The burden of holding on to my past hurts had brought on so much fear and distress that I had to learn to forgive. This was not at all easy for me, because I had to forgive the one who hurt me. I had to forgive the one who harmed me, betrayed me, and mistreated me. Prior to learning the benefit of forgiveness, according to the Word of God, I never thought about forgiving him. Actually, I was comfortable with being angry towards him, but I had to forgive him, because Jesus has forgiven me. It is clearly stated in Matthew 18:21 that I must forgive those that sin against me. This is a matter that I had no choice in. I understand now that I must always walk in forgiveness and keep on forgiving because the advantage belongs to me. I had to first be healed in this area, as I released this issue and this person and give it all to God. I began to focus on the promises of God and not my past hurts and pains. I did finally realize that there was nothing that this man could do to undo the hurt or the pain that I experienced. Quiet frankly, Marcus can't repay me because he doesn't even owe me anything. I have canceled that debt in the name of Jesus. I had to forgive him in order for me to move forward with my life. When I forgave him, this allowed me to be in a place of peace and joy. My journey was very difficult, as I consulted with professionals and attended many counseling sessions. If you are in need of help, please seek counseling, a safe place, and/or legal assistance during your recovery stage. I needed to build my relationship with God, as I have found my greatest joy in serving Him and being in His will. I do thank God for keeping me in His secret place and under His wing of protection. I do recognize that I could not have done this in my own strength; I began to understand that He covered me daily. I now have a fresh supply of strength and enjoyment. I am assured that the Lord kept me to do His work and that entails being a good wife to my husband, a Proverbs 31 wife.

A Wife of Noble Character

Who can find a virtuous and capable wife?
She is more precious than rubies.
Her husband can trust her,
and she will greatly enrich his life.
She brings him good, not harm,
all the days of her life.
She finds wool and flax
and busily spins it.
She is like a merchant's ship,
bringing her food from afar.
She gets up before dawn to prepare breakfast for her household
and plan the day's work for her servant girls.
She goes to inspect a field and buys it;

with her earnings she plants a vineyard.
She is energetic and strong,
a hard worker.
She makes sure her dealings are profitable;
her lamp burns late into the night.
Her hands are busy spinning thread,
her fingers twisting fiber.
She extends a helping hand to the poor
and opens her arms to the needy.
She has no fear of winter for her household,
for everyone has warm clothes.
She makes her own bedspreads.
She dresses in fine linen and purple gowns.
Her husband is well known at the city gates,
where he sits with the other civic leaders.
She makes belted linen garments
and sashes to sell to the merchants.
She is clothed with strength and dignity,
and she laughs without fear of the future.
When she speaks, her words are wise,
and she gives instructions with kindness.
She carefully watches everything in her household
and suffers nothing from laziness.
Her children stand and bless her.
Her husband praises her:
"There are many virtuous and capable women in the world,
but you surpass them all!"
Charm is deceptive, and beauty does not last;
but a woman who fears the LORD will be greatly praised.
Reward her for all she has done.
Let her deeds publicly declare her praise.

God kept me to be a good mother to my children, to guide and provide for them; a daughter and friend to my mother, by supporting her and lifting her up with prayer through the hard times. I am called to be a good sister to my siblings, advising and guiding them while letting my light shine. Many people have asked me why I continued in an abusive relationship for so long and others have asked me how I overcame so much heart ache and pain. I tell them that I have learned that God is true to His Word, God's Word works, and God's Word works for me. He has always worked out the details in my life, right down to the why, the who, and the how of any situation, as I lean on and trust in Him. Who you choose to lean on will determine your destiny. I am in a place were I have repented for my sins and I have been delivered in order to minister to the people, which God has placed in my life. In that past season, I had to cry many nights. In that season I had to lose, I had to hate my life enough to die to old desires and resist temptations of the flesh. I had to keep silent many times. But now....Now I am in my season of joy! With God's grace I lived through all the life threatening behaviors and I survived all the physical attacks. I am building myself up daily with God's help. In this season I am now laughing and rejoicing.

Those tears of sorrow and fear are now tears of joy and peace!
I am now smiling from the inside out.
I have so much joy and peace in my life.
Yes, this is my season.
This is the season for me to be the best me.
This is the season for me to love me and I know that God loves me.

What season is this for you? Take a moment to reflect back with me. I think about all the things that I did wrong. I remember being in all the wrong places and socializing with all the wrong people. I think of the friends that I thought I had and the love that I tried to have. I was trying to make friends and force love when in fact all I was doing was loosing myself in the process of looking for love and acceptance. I have heard so many people say that experience is the best teacher. Wow! How I wish, I could wish that pain away. Now, experience did teach me some things, but these are some lessons that I'm sure I could have survived without! I have talked to many women that have gotten caught up in abusive relationships. They are looking for what they think love should look like or what they have heard love should feel like. The idea of a man taking care of us is just an innate desire that a lot of women have. We like that security and the thought of a man providing that material means of support. Now, I understand the importance of him having a job and paying the bills, but does this give him the right to mistreat you and abuse you? Sure it's a good thing that the bills are paid, but there must be balance! For a man to be the head of the house is by design, but this all falls under the covenant of the marriage vows. The relationship and abuse that I referenced in this book, was all from my perspective of a sinner saved by the grace of God.

I know that it may be fashionable today to say "I will not settle for a man without a J-O-B!" We lay out his material attributes, because he needs to have a car and employment. And good credit is definitely a plus! What does any of these things matter, if he spending money on you during the day and putting his hands on you at night. Too many of us are focused on his money and his car, but not focused on ourselves and our future. We tell ourselves that we don't want to be alone, so we sit and we do nothing. We miss the joy of the new day. We blame ourselves for the unhappiness in our relationships and no matter how pretty the sun shines, we complain about how hot it is. The snowflakes fall on an early December morning, but we complain about how cold it is. This is the day that the Lord has made, let us rejoice and be glad in it. Often times women in abusive relationships are made to think they can not have an opinion on any important decision making. They believe that that their feelings don't count, so they put these feelings in their pockets, just to keep them from getting hurt. We often put our deepest desires on a shelf, hoping to be able to come back and pick them up later, allowing the man to degrade us all in the name of love.

"Where was the love?"

"Where was the respect?"

It's almost like being an exotic dancer. A man throws a few dollars at your feet and you move anyway he wants you to. You close your eyes and pretend that you are in another place, during another time, doing something different. But ladies open your eyes to the reality of the situation. You are now standing in a place of humiliation, with a few dollars at your feet to shut you up and pay the light bill. There I stood exposed and humiliated in front of a man not even worthy of the view. I was stripped of all the values and had abandoned all the little lessons that mamma tried to teach me as a child. I remembered that feeling of embarrassment, worthlessness and I asked myself... .."How did I let it get to this point?" A lot of women began to blame themselves and start with the should've, would've, could've points, but it is okay. The time is over where we have to live a masqueraded life. Take your mask off and look at your situation. It is time to flip that situation and get a new start. I want you to learn how to turn that thing around and get in the Word of God and allow that Word to minister to you. Don't be hard on yourself, please allow adequate time to get over that man and take time to heal. We all have areas that we need to work on and a lot of growing to do. As we grow, we will allow God's word to speak to our hearts. Continue to read His Word, be true to his word, but most of all be true to yourself. We can now move forward and stop living life from the outside in, masquerading around pretending to be okay. We can stop buying expensive clothes and expensive jewelry just to cover up that pain. A lot of women are trying to look good on the outside, but are all torn up on the inside. Ladies, I know we spend a lot of time and money into making all those adjustments. We are constantly trying to cover up hurt and hide pain that is still there. It is sad to say, but the truth is that there are many women who are still living with an abusive husband or boyfriend. There are many other women right now that are battling with past child abuse or molestation. It is so shameful, because we have carried these hurts for so long, while still trying to move on with our lives. We are trying to add families and careers on top of problems that we never dealt with or never addressed, we just covered them up. If this sounds like you, I'm sure that this unresolved hurt has only made your loads heavier. I urge each of you to take a moment to think about what you are carrying. What all have you added to the load that you were already carrying? My dear sisters, it is time to come to a drop off point. I come in agreement with you, as you drop those problems off, those disappointments and frustrations. It may not be easy, but these tasks are not impossible, trust God and drop that abusive man off with God, He will cover you, protect you, and strengthen you!

I will not worry about anything. I will pray and wait with thanksgiving and trust God to cover my marriage, my children, and my finances. And the peace of God, which surpasses what I understand, will keep my heart and mind. Amen (Philippians 4:6)

Now drop to your knees and thank God for your break through.

I cast my anxiety on Him, because He cares for me. (1 Peter 5:7).

"Because you love me", says the Lord, "I will rescue you, I will protect you, for you acknowledge my name. (Psalm 91:14)

Healing is a process and it does not occur overnight. It takes time, but with God all things are possible. As horrible and as painful as this was for me, this experience helped me to grow through some things! I recognized my strength and my potential. This was a very hard lesson for me, but it helped to shape my attitude and my beliefs. I was standing at an apple tree, waiting for it to produce oranges. I was cornered between death and defeat, but I have now moved from fear to freedom. I have learned to develop my prayer life and to speak to my situation; whatever that situation may be, and I tell my situation what it will be according to the Word of God. There is so much strength in scripture!

Today, I encourage you to read these scriptures and allow them to speak to your heart. Daily you should plead the promises of God over your life and the life of your family.

Precious Promises:

Because you are precious in My sight and honored, and because I love you, I will give men in return for you and peoples in exchange for your life (Isaiah 43:4).

As for God, His way is perfect! The word of the Lord is tested and tried; He is a shield to all those who take refuge and put their trust in Him (Psalm 18:30).

Whatever I ask for in prayer, I believe that I have received it, and it will be mine (Mark 11:24).

The LORD is my light and my salvation—whom shall I fear? The LORD is the stronghold of my life—of whom shall I be afraid? (Psalm 27:1).

Let your gentleness be evident to all. The Lord is near. Do not be anxious about anything, but in everything, by prayer and petition, with thanksgiving, present your requests to God. And the peace of God, which transcends all understanding, will guard your hearts and your minds in Christ Jesus (Philippians 4:5-7).

"Come to me, all you who are weary and burdened, and I will give you rest. Take my yoke upon you and learn from me, for I am gentle and humble in heart, and you will find rest for your souls. For my yoke is easy and my burden is light." (Matthew 11:28-30).

Then you will call, and the LORD will answer; you will cry for help, and he will say: Here am I. (Isaiah 58:9).

When I am afraid, I will trust in you. In God, whose word I praise, in God I trust; I will not be afraid. What can man do to me? (Psalm 56:3-4).

May the God of hope fill you with all joy and peace as you trust in him, so that you may overflow with hope by the power of the Holy Spirit. (Romans 15:13).

But I tell you who hear me: Love your enemies, do good to those who hate you, bless those who curse you, pray for those who mistreat you (Luke 6:27-28).

He sends forth His word and heals them and rescues them from the pit and destruction (Psalm 107:20).

This Book of the Law shall not depart out of your mouth, but you shall meditate on it day and night, that you may observe and do accordingly to all that is written in it. For then you shall make your way prosperous, and then you shall deal wisely and have good success (Joshua 1:8).

Beloved, I pray that you may prosper in every way and that your body may keep well, even as your soul keeps well and prospers (3 John 1:2).

Chapter 13

A New Day!

Therefore, if anyone is in Christ, he is a new creation; the old has gone, the new has come (2 Corinthians 5:17)!

As I reflect back on my past, I can see things so differently now. I was saved, but not doing saved things. I confessed Jesus as my Lord and Savior as a child. I had accepted Christ and I knew about all His great works; yet I was a backslider, saved by grace and riding on the prayers of my family. The enemy tried to steal my joy, destroy my peace, and kill me, but Jesus came for me to have and enjoy life. I believed in God and I kept hoping and praying, but even then, I continued to live in sin. But, through it all I knew that I could trust God. I knew that I could cast all my cares on Him. I knew that I had fallen and I knew that He was my only chance to get back up. I carried the hurt and the pain for to many years. It took me a long time to forgive and even longer to be healed, but once I found love, true love, the love of God, I knew that I finally found peace. Are you looking for peace, love, and joy? He is the complete expression of love! Are you looking for a love that will offer you more than your earthly father ever could? If you seek Him with all your heart you will find a love that is ever lasting. He is a provider that will provide and give you a future filled with hopes and dreams.

I am now stepping high and walking in my new, through faith in God and belief in myself! I thank God that I am no longer struggling with yesterday's little girl and no longer mentally involved with wounds from my past. That little girl with those little wishes has grown into a woman of integrity and virtue. I walked out my fiery furnace with some scars and some burns, but through my spiritual transformation and Godly revelation, there is no residue. I don't have an excess of pain, hurt, lust, or lies holding me down. I had to make some wise choices about how to live and love. I learned to see my life through God's perspective and I thank God for giving me the strength to leave.

I made a decision that I would not allow that part of my life to determine who I am or who I will be. I now know what love is and therefore I give love. I am inspired to reach the full potential God gave me. The problems won't just go away, but you can cast all your cares on Him. As you learn to trust Him, He will order your steps and direct your paths. I thank God for the joy and peace that only He can give.

To God be the glory, I have a New Story. I am as blessed as I look; I have an abundance of peace and joy. I still coordinate my accessories well with my attire, my hair is together, and yes my nails are manicured. I dress it up on the outside, but I have learned to clothe and prep my inside daily, my spiritual man. Do you put on the full armor of God, so that you can take your stand against the devil's schemes? For you see, our struggles are not against flesh and blood, but against the rulers, against the authorities, against the powers of the dark world and against the spiritual forces of evil in the heavenly realms (Ephesians 6:11).

Do you dress each day according to the weather, so that you can be prepared for rain, sleet, or snow? Do you watch the news and listen as the weatherman reports? He says that the forecast reads mostly cloudy with an 80% chance of rain. This report helps us to prepare for the next day. I usually select my wardrobe according to the news report and I often lay my clothes out the night before. I'm sure most of you still lay your clothes out the night before, hoping to get an early start on your day. This weather report, you see is how we determine our wardrobe, and many of us still check the news the next morning just to be sure. We grab our umbrellas and we head out the door, prepared for our next move! So, as you look at your situation, your report may read some fear and frustration. And though you have prepared for your next move, the attacks will still come. But you must hold on to that B-I-B-L-E, which tells you that no weapon formed against you, shall prosper. As you step out your door, the forecast reads recession and depression. Whose report will you believe? I am shielded from these things you see, because I have on my Ephesians Word! I am standing firm, with the belt of truth buckled around my waist, the breastplate of righteousness in place, and my feet fitted with readiness that comes from the gospel of peace. In addition to all this, I take up the shield of faith, which I can now extinguish all the flaming arrows of the evil one. I will take the helmet of salvation and the sword of the Spirit, which is the Word of God.

I pray that for those of you who are in an abusive relationship or dealing with any types of fear, frustrations, insecurities, or depression will seek the help that you need and grab hold to the "Truth," which is the Word of God. I urge you to take advantage of the community resources that are available to you, and find those that offer a safe and secure environment. My hope is that my experiences and my testimonies inform, inspire, and encourage you to seek the things of God. I have chosen to make better choices, so that I can live my life to the fullest and in abundance. This is my love and I chose to love God first, my husband and my family. I have learned to protect my love and guard my heart, as I strive to be the best me that I can be. There are many scriptures revealed to you throughout this text. These precious promises are an illustration for you and me to see that throughout our disappointments and mistakes His promises remained the same. His Word never changed! His Word was and is always available to you and to me no matter what we are going through or what issues we are dealing with!

I am no longer bound by worldly expectations. I do not search for happiness or look for love. I am not intimidated by false love and not impressed with material gain. I refuse to fall in love with things, because material things have a tendency to come in and take over our attitudes, our relationships, and our values if we allow it. I now realize that I am not prosperous because of the things that I have. I am prosperous because of the life that I live! Those material things that I loved and held on to for so many years handicapped me and desensitized my character. I have learned to love Jesus and enjoy the things. Seek ye first the kingdom and His righteousness and all these things will be added (Matthew 6:33). I still enjoy the good life, but I do not put worldly possessions before God. I know that God's mercies are new each and every day, and I do my best to make the most of these days. I once had someone ask me what I was so happy about, and now that you know my story, you understand that I now walk in His glory! I have made that shift from lust to love. I had to admit to my insecurities, my confusion, and my childhood pain. I had to repent for my sinful desires and my sexual soul ties. I salute each of you who have taken a stand against Domestic Violence. I pray that we continue to help others to heal as we restore the kingdom of God.

I am healed.

I am delivered.

I am prosperous.

I have begun to spend more time in the Word of God. I learned that I must read the Word in order to know what He says about my life. As I began to apply Godly principles, I began to see my life line up with how God originally intended for it to be! I have been experiencing God's power and glory like never before. As you pray your way through, began to develop a new attitude as revelation comes and you discover the life that God has planned for you. Make no excuses and take no detours on this new journey!

We all need someone to support and encourage us as we embark on our new journey and transition into our destinies. I must say that I am very grateful to have a mother that loved me through all my chaos and confusion. I have been very blessed, because in spite of all my trials and tribulations, she encouraged me to live out my dreams. She believed in me, and I thank God for the many words of wisdom that she spoke over me. I thank her for all the time she gave and all love that she shared. Her continued support and understanding helped me to get back on track and recommit my life. My mother truly impacted my life. She always had a working spirit and a word of encouragement. From her I learned that there are no limits placed on us, but the ones that we place on ourselves. "The sky is the limit". She trained me up in the way that I needed to go and though I departed from it, I am now back on track. I am finally at peace with myself and my past. And though my father wasn't there for me, my mother was my inspiration that pushed me to be the best me. My daddy died when I was in boot camp and I remember that day like it was yesterday. I was upset because I never said "I love you" and torn because I never got to say goodbye.

It took me a long time to understand the turmoil of my past, but as I accepted my insecurities I was able to move on and be strong. I am now enjoying life with God, my husband and my two beautiful children. Despite my adversities and my past lifestyle, I know that I am a good wife and an outstanding mother. That path was a journey that taught me to stand firm, remain strong, and be very courageous when faced with immeasurable obstacles and unsure outcomes. And though sometimes I still don't understand the many adversities that come my way, I do understand that I must trust God.

Precious Promise:

We are pressed on every side by troubles, but we are not crushed. We are perplexed, but not driven to despair. We are hunted down, but never abandoned by God. We get knocked down, but we are not destroyed. Through suffering, our bodies continue to share in the death of Jesus so that the life of Jesus may also be seen in our bodies (2 Corinthians 4:8).

I did not take time to get to know the man who would always love me. I didn't know that God could love a sinner like me. I had done so many wrong things. I had hurt so many people and I had told plenty of lies. "How could I go to God with all this mess?" But the truth is, He already knew about my disorderly conduct and He loved me anyway. I had to realize that God loves me just the way I am. I came to Him at the lowest point of my life and I didn't have to fix up any of my mess ups. I didn't have to wait until I got things right. I just realized that in Him is love. He is my love, my happiness, and my peace. I no longer had to hide it. I no longer had to pretend. I was free to love Him openly and consistently. All my sins have been forgiven and all my debts paid. For God so loved the world that He gave His one and only Son, that whoever believes in Him shall not perish but have eternal life (John 3:16). Jesus is the love of my life. All I had to do was open my mouth and confess that He is Lord and I believed in my heart. I repented for my sins and He has gradually removed each and every burden that I carried for so many years. I am proud of me and I am aware of who I am. Ladies, you don't need a man to validate you or prove his love to you. Whoever does not love, does not know God, because God is love. (1 John 4:8).

If you receive the gift of my son Jesus, you receive me.
1 John 2:23

And nothing will ever separate you from my love again.
Romans 8:38-39

Ask yourself, "Is it safe for me to stay?" "Is it time for a change?" Change is good, but it starts with you taking a step towards your freedom. Educate yourself about domestic violence, the statistics of domestic relationships, and research your options. We fear failure, but to do nothing is to fail for sure!

I am now a stronger and a better woman and I have learned that……

Love does not hurt.
Love is not rude.
Love is not loud and disrespectful.
Love is not money and arrogance.
Love is not control and deceit.
Love is not fearful and demeaning.
Love is like a sweet fragrance that never looses its smell.
Love is a dim smile, just because you entered the room.
Love is that pat on the back to say, job well done.
Love is sharing and caring.
I now know what love is.
I now know what true love is and I now understand that I must love me first, before I can love anyone else!

-Kamekio Danielle Lewis

How do we break the cycle of abuse?

Research shows that domestic violence is the number one health issue for women. It accounts for 20% of all medical visits for women and 25% of emergency room visits. Domestic violence has a huge impact on you, the victim, your family and your friends. There is help available to help restore you and to help support you as you make this transition. We must realize that we have the power to end this. We have to recognize the warning signs and understand that the first and most important step is taking control and taking action in of our situation. I do understand that we can't just focus on how to get out, but where can I go and who is going to keep me safe? They are many women in these domestic violence situations and are so gripped by fear they are so afraid to leave. How can I get out and stay out? Please seek out help in your local community or call one of the numbers I have listed below, again my book is for inspiration and support, not a substitute for professional advice. - www.breakthecycle.org

Facts:

- ☐ October is Domestic Violence Month
- ☐ 95% of the victims are female.
- ☐ 95-98% of the perpetrators are male.
- ☐ Every 15 seconds a woman is beaten, raped, or killed.
- ☐ Domestic violence occurs among all racial, ethnic, religious, and socioeconomic groups.
- ☐ Battering is the largest single major cause of injury to women.
- ☐ Everyday, 4 women are murdered at the hands of an intimate partner.
- ☐ About 2 - 4 million American women are battered each year by their partners.
- ☐ Women are at a 75% greater risk of being killed after they leave their partners.
- ☐ About 1/3 of female homicide victims are killed by their partners.

- ☐ Boys who have witnessed abuse of their mothers are twice as likely to abuse their female partners and children as adults.
- ☐ Children who witness domestic violence are more likely to commit sexual assault crimes.
- ☐ Between 3 and 10 million American children witness domestic violence each year.
- ☐ Children of abused mothers are more likely to attempt suicide, abuse drugs and alcohol, run away from home, and engage in teenage prostitution.
- ☐ In a 1992 study, 63% of imprisoned kids between ages 11 – 20 were doing time for killing their mother's batterer.
- ☐ Statistics show that the majority of abusers where abused themselves.

www.turningpointservices.org

Useful Information

- 1-800-799-Safe (7223) - 24 hour National Domestic Hotline
- 1-800-787-3224 (TTY)
- 1-866-331-9474 – National Teen Dating Abuse Helpline
- 1-866-331-8453 TTY
- 1-888-792-2873 – Family Violence Prevention Fund
- 1-800-903-0111 ext. 3 - Battered Women's Justice Project
- National Battered Women's Law Project
  275 7th Avenue, Suite 1206
  New York, NY 10001
  Phone: 212-741-9480
  FAX: 212-741-6438
- More information on domestic violence
  www.ndvh.org
  www.abusedwoman.com
  http://www.acadv.org/dating.html
  www.loveisnotabuse.com

You may be in an emotionally abusive relationship if your partner:

- Calls you names
- Insults you or continually criticizes you
- Tries to keep you from your friends and family
- Monitors where you go, who you call and who you spend time with
- Threatens to hurt you, the children, or your family

You may be in a physical abusive relationship if your partner has ever:

- Damaged property, when angry (thrown objects, punched walls, or kicked doors)
- Pushed, slapped, bitten, kicked, or choked you
- Abandoned you in a dangerous or unfamiliar place
- Scared you by driving recklessly
- Used a weapon to threaten or hurt you

You may be in a sexually abusive relationship if your partner:

- Insults you in sexual ways or calls you sexual names
- Has ever forced or manipulated you into having sex or performing sexual acts
- Held you down during sex
- Demanded sex when you were sick, tired or after beating you

www.helpguide.org/.../domestic_violence_abuse_types_signs_causes_effects.htm

Sources

LeRoux, William and Douglas, Lynette, 2003. Promises from God for Women

Mills, Linda G. 2003. Insult to Injury: Rethinking our response to intimate abuse

Rogers, Sheila A. 2002. From fear to Freedom: Abused wives find hope and healing.

About the Author

Kamekio Danielle has a passion to share the love of God through ministry and fellowship with women and children. She will share with you her intimate story about her journey of life, loving, and living. Her sincere hope is that her experiences and testimonies will inform, inspire, and encourage you to seek the things of God.

A native of Camden, Arkansas, Kamekio has always provided a support system and listening ear to so many of her family and friends. She graduated from Camden Fairview High School in 1995 and ventured on to the University of Arkansas at Pine Bluff, majoring in Social Work. She had an unexpected twist in her life and after graduating from the University of Arkansas at Pine Bluff, she joined the United States Army. She received orders that would take her all the way to Ft. Wainwright, Alaska, where she stayed for three years and meet her husband Dennis Lewis. The couple married March 10, 2001 in Fairbanks, Alaska and later had two children together, Kaveyon Lewis (8 years old) and Kemareyon Lewis (6 years old). Kamekio currently holds a Masters of Education from Auburn University, she is a graduate from Ministry Training International, (Memphis, TN) and an active member of Alpha Kappa Alpha Sorority.

"I will not forget my past, I understand my present, but I'm focusing on my future."

--**Kamekio Lewis**

For those of you, who wish to write letters to Kamekio, please feel free to do so. For any other inquires, book signings or speaking engagements, please email: kamekio@bellsouth.net

Looking for Love
3125 S. Mendenall Suite 230
Memphis, TN 38115

CPSIA information can be obtained at www.ICGtesting.com
Printed in the USA
LVOW060442230911

247526LV00001B/4/P